LAUBACH WAY TO
Reading 2

A time-tested method that has taught millions of adults to read

TEACHER'S EDITION

IN HONOR OF

Elizabeth (Betty) Mooney Kirk

1914–2004

Co-author of *Laubach Way to Reading*

FRANK C. LAUBACH • ELIZABETH MOONEY KIRK • ROBERT S. LAUBACH

New Readers Press
ProLiteracy's publishing division

Laubach Way to Reading
Teacher's Edition 2
ISBN 978-1-56420-922-1

Copyright © 2011, 1991, 1981 New Readers Press
New Readers Press
A Publishing Division of ProLiteracy
104 Marcellus Street, Syracuse, New York 13204
www.newreaderspress.com

Printed in the United States of America
9   8   7   6   5   4   3

Proceeds from the sale of New Readers Press materials support professional
development, training, and technical assistance programs of ProLiteracy
that benefit local literacy programs in the U.S. and around the globe.

Developmental Editor: Terrie Lipke
Creative Director: Andrea Woodbury
Production Specialist: Maryellen Casey
Art and Design Supervisor: James P. Wallace
Illustrations: Tom McNeely and Drew Rose, represented by Wilkinson Studios, Inc.
Cover Design: Carolyn Wallace

Table of Contents

Series Overview 5
Introduction to Book 2 7
Scope and Sequence 8
Lesson Notes Overview 10
Lesson Notes for Book 2 11

LESSON 1: Book 2, pages 6–9 11
I. Reading 11
II. Skills Practice 14
III. Writing 14

LESSON 2: Book 2, pages 10–15 17
I. Reading 17
II. Skills Practice 19
III. Writing 20

LESSON 3: Book 2, pages 16–19 23
I. Reading 23
II. Skills Practice 25
III. Writing 25

LESSON 4: Book 2, pages 20–25 27
I. Reading 27
II. Skills Practice 28
III. Writing 29

LESSON 5: Book 2, pages 26–29 31
I. Reading 31
II. Skills Practice 33
III. Writing 33

LESSON 6: Book 2, pages 30–35 35
I. Reading 35
II. Skills Practice 36
III. Writing 37

LESSON 7: Book 2, pages 36–39 39
I. Reading 39
II. Skills Practice 40
III. Writing 41

LESSON 8: Book 2, pages 40–45 43
I. Reading 43
II. Skills Practice 45
III. Writing 45

LESSON 9: Book 2, pages 46–51 47
I. Reading 47
II. Skills Practice 47
III. Writing 49

LESSON 10: Book 2, pages 52–57 51
I. Reading 51
II. Skills Practice 53
III. Writing 54

LESSON 11: Book 2, pages 58–63 57
I. Reading 57
II. Skills Practice 59
III. Writing 61

LESSON 12: Book 2, pages 64–69 63
I. Reading 63
II. Skills Practice 65
III. Writing 67

LESSON 13: Book 2, pages 70–73 68
I. Reading 68
II. Skills Practice 69
III. Writing 71

LESSON 14: Book 2, pages 74–78 72
I. Reading in *City Living,* Pages 5–12 72
II. Skills Practice 73
III. Writing 75

LESSON 15: Book 2, pages 79–82 76
I. Reading in *City Living,* Pages 13–23 76
II. Skills Practice 76
III. Writing 77

Checkups for Book 2 79
Word List for Book 2 82

Series Overview

Laubach Way to Reading is a basic reading and writing series developed primarily for adults with little or no reading ability. The series consists of four levels with student skill books, workbooks, and correlated readers for student use. The teacher's edition for each level gives detailed instructions and lesson plans.

The series provides a systematic development of basic reading and writing skills. Each lesson includes vocabulary development, phonic or structural analysis of words, the reading of a short story, comprehension checks, and writing practice. The lessons progress from the sounds and regular spellings of basic consonants to those of the short vowels, the long vowels, and finally the irregular spellings and more difficult reading, writing, and grammar skills.

The student skill books, workbooks, and readers may be used both with English speakers and with those who are learning English. A separate series of manuals, *Laubach Way to English*, provides complete instructions for teaching the skills of listening, speaking, reading, and writing English to the non-English-speaking student.

Although designed primarily for adults, *Laubach Way to Reading* may also be used successfully with high school dropouts or students in intermediate grades who need remedial work in basic reading, writing, or spelling. Classroom teachers, teacher aides, and volunteer tutors may all use the books effectively.

Book 1: Sounds and Names of Letters

Beginning on a zero level, book 1 lays an essential foundation in word attack and comprehension skills. The name and one sound for each letter of the alphabet and the digraphs *ch, sh,* and *th* are introduced. Simple sentence patterns encourage fluency in reading. Blending of sounds, punctuation, silent reading, and manuscript writing are introduced. A total of 132 words is used.

Book 2: Short Vowel Sounds

Lessons are structured around the short vowel sounds, *y* as a vowel as in *city,* and the *r*-controlled vowel sounds for *er, ir, ur,* and *ar.* The digraphs *ng* and *wh* are introduced, as are beginning and ending consonant blends. Simple skills of punctuation, structural analysis, comprehension, and sentence writing are introduced. A total of 192 new words is introduced.

Book 3: Long Vowel Sounds

This book presents the long sounds for *a, e, i,* and *o* with their regular spellings, one regular spelling for long *u,* and the sound for *or* as in *York.* Comprehension skills include finding main ideas, summarizing content, recognizing implied meaning, developing opinions, and predicting outcomes. Lessons include functional materials like ads, bills, menus, letters, and checks. A total of 399 new words is used.

Cursive writing is taught at this level. For this, the student needs the cursive writing workbook, and the teacher needs the cursive writing teacher's guide.

Book 4: Other Vowel Sounds and Consonant Spellings

This book continues with the regular spellings for the long *u* sound and goes on to the letter combinations *oo, ou, aw, oi,* and their variant spellings. The book also covers different sounds represented by the same consonant symbol, such as the *s* in *see* and *please,* and regular spellings for consonant sounds that may be spelled in more than one way, such as the /k/ sound in *keep* and *can.*

Word analysis skills are strengthened by more work with contractions and compound words and by the student's becoming familiar with the most common prefixes and suffixes. Practice is given to increase reading speed.

Comprehension skills emphasized include making inferences, identifying cause and effect, drawing conclusions, and understanding the mood and atmosphere of a story. Also, students are helped to interpret the author's opinions and to evaluate their own reactions to what they read.

Correlated Readers

The correlated reader for each level is a collection of stories or articles using much of the same vocabulary as the skill book. The correlated readers are an intrinsic part of the series as they provide opportunity for the student to gain confidence and independent reading habits.

Supplementary Materials

Laubach Way to Reading Workbooks complement the skill books and provide additional practice in reading, writing, listening, and speaking. Workbook vocabulary is correlated to each level, and some new words are introduced. These workbooks are helpful to both native and non-native English speakers who are learning basic reading and writing skills.

The *More Stories* books offer additional reading at levels 1–4. These engaging stories feature characters from the *Laubach Way to Reading* books, and reinforce the new vocabulary learned at each level.

Focus on Phonics uses a word-pattern approach to teach word-attack skills. Vocabulary is correlated to the *Laubach Way to Reading* levels.

Puzzles 1 & 2 and *Puzzles 3 & 4* feature vocabulary and spelling practice within an assortment of word scrambles, word searches, and crossword puzzles at each level.

The Laubach Way to Cursive Writing uses vocabulary and sentence structures from level 3 to teach students to write in cursive. The teacher's guide includes step-by-step instructions to ensure success.

A few other components are available online, such as Checkups, Student Profiles and Diagnostic Inventory, and Diplomas. To print copies, go to www.newreaderspress.com.

Principles on Which Laubach Lessons Are Based

Establishing letter-sound relationships. The letters of the alphabet and the sounds they stand for are taught in a systematic manner. This series uses existing phonetic regularities, emphasizes regular spellings, and provides aids to irregular spellings.

Learning through association. Letters and sounds are presented through key words with picture associations.

Moving from the known to the unknown. The student starts with the spoken word, which he knows, and moves in short steps to the written word, which he does not know.

Familiar vocabulary. Words used are in the spoken vocabulary of the adult. Vocabulary is controlled, with a limited number of new words in each lesson.

Use of repetition to strengthen the visual image. Each word and sentence pattern is repeated several times soon after it is taught.

Use of meaningful content. From the beginning, reading for meaning is stressed.

Something new in each lesson. Each lesson teaches something new in a familiar lesson pattern.

Independence in learning. Visual aids, phonic skills, consistent lesson patterns, and uniformity of format make it easy for the student to help himself.

Learning reading and writing together. Correlation of reading and writing in each lesson helps to reinforce skills. Also, the student is highly motivated when he can progress in writing along with reading.

Lessons are easy to teach. The lessons are planned for maximum self-help and minimum teacher help. The detailed manuals for teachers make it possible for inexperienced teachers to use the materials successfully.

Research on English Language Applied to This Series

The English alphabet has 26 letters which are used to express 43 sounds. The five letters called vowels represent at least 18 different sounds. The 25 consonant sounds are represented by 21 letters. So a major problem with English is that there are not enough alphabetic symbols to represent the sounds of the language.

The chart below shows the regular spelling of vowel sounds in *Laubach Way to Reading*. Generally, the vowel sounds are taught in the order of frequency of use. When vowel sounds are spelled in more than one way, the spellings that occur most frequently are taught first.

REGULAR SPELLING OF VOWEL SOUNDS

	Sound	Examples	Regular Spelling
Short Vowels	i	in	i
	y	lily	y
	u	up	u
	e	egg	e
	a	apple	a
	o	olive	o
	er	fern, burn, bird	er, ur, ir
	ar	arms	ar
Long Vowels	ā	paper, day, paint, cake	a, ay, ai, a-e
	ē	we, tree, eat, key, Pete	e, ee, ea, ey, e-e
	ī, ȳ	I, my, tie, night, time	i, y, ie, igh, i-e
	ō, or	go, boat, snow, York, home	o, oa, ow, or, o-e
	ū	music, argue, few, cure	u, ue, ew, u-e
Other Vowels	ū *or* oo	news, due, tuition	ew, ue, u
	oo	moon	oo
	uu	book	oo
	ou	cloud, town	ou, ow
	aw	auto, paw, all, walk	au, aw, a(ll), a(lk)
		bought	ough(t)
	oi	oil, boy	oi, oy

Introduction to Book 2

Lessons in book 2 reinforce the sounds and letters introduced in book 1. A few new sounds are introduced. Except for the sight words learned in book 1 and two new words used in exercises, only words with short vowel sounds are used. The student is expected to apply phonics skills in reading new words. More word recognition, comprehension, writing, and spelling skills are introduced.

You may use the Scope and Sequence chart as a guide to your student's progress. It is important for him to master the sounds for the consonants and short vowels by the end of the book.

Materials Needed for This Level

Book 2 contains 15 lessons. Each of the first 12 lessons contains a chart, story, writing lesson, and homework page. Each lesson teaches one vowel sound.

The chart presents the vowel sound being taught and several words with that sound. The chart is divided into four columns. Column 1 has a picture. Column 2 has the word for the picture. Column 3 identifies the different sounds in the word to help the student pronounce it. Column 4 repeats the word with its correct spelling.

In column 3 of the chart, each sound in the word is represented by one letter or two letters together. Spelling is changed only for the part of the word in which a sound is not regularly spelled with a spelling pattern previously taught or being taught in that lesson. Space is left between the letter or letters representing the individual sounds to aid the student in identifying each sound.

The story uses the chart words. Any other new words introduced in the story are listed at the top of the page. The new words are respelled where necessary to aid the student in pronunciation. The writing lessons and homework assignments are correlated with the reading lessons, helping the student to spell the words he has learned to read. Listen-and-write exercises give practice in writing words and later sentences from dictation.

The correlated reader *City Living* is introduced in Lesson 14. (Replicas are not included in this manual.)

Checkups for level 2, available on our website, should be administered after the student completes book 2 to help evaluate his progress in reading and writing.Directions for administering these checkups follow the lesson plans in this manual.

More Stories 2 and *Focus on Phonics* may be used as supplements to meet individual needs. Suggestions for their use are in the lesson plans.

Schedule

In most cases, a student can cover a lesson in an hour session. He will probably need an additional half hour for the homework. A student who has two sessions a week should be able to complete the skill book, correlated reader, and checkups in 10 or 12 weeks. It is important, however, that he cover each lesson and not skip through the skill book. The lessons are systematically arranged to give him a foundation of independent reading skills.

General Plan for the Lessons

The major steps in the lesson presentation for this skill book may be summarized as follows:

1. Introduce the vowel in the chart for the lesson. Let the student read the key word and identify the vowel sound with its letter symbol.

2. Guide the student through the chart so that he moves from the picture to the word, to the identification of letter-sound relationships, to the word again. After the first chart is explained, he may be able to read many of the charts independently. You can give help where needed.

3. Have the student go over the new words in the story before reading it. He will usually be able to pronounce them by himself as their sounds have already been taught.

4. Have the student read silently. Direct his reading and check his comprehension with oral questions.

5. Have the student read the story or part of it orally.

6. Relate the story to his experience through questions in the Reading between the Lines section of the lesson notes.

7. Provide exercises for auditory discrimination that will also help the student generalize about sound-letter relationships. These will aid him in spelling and pronunciation. Suggestions for these and other exercises on adding endings to words are in the Skills Practice section of each lesson plan.

8. Check the homework assignment from the previous lesson before the student begins the Writing section of the lesson.

9. In the Writing Lessons, help the student study the spelling of new words, calling attention to special points. In the listen-and-write exercises, encourage careful listening and dictate words which have regular sound-letter relationships.

10. Go over the new homework assignment to make sure that the student understands what to do.

Meeting Individual Needs

If a student needs to move at a slower pace, you may present a supplementary lesson at intervals, similar to the one suggested in Appendix A of *Teacher's Edition 1*. More supplementary exercises are in the lesson plans, along with suggestions for independent study.

A student who finds book 2 very easy may move through it at a more rapid pace. But be sure he masters all the skills and can recognize most of the words.

Scope and Sequence
SKILLS INTRODUCED OR REINFORCED IN BOOK 2

Phonics skills	Lesson	1	2	3	4	5	6	7	8	9	10	11	12	13	14	15
1. Recognize the short sound for vowels:	*i*	•	•	•	•	•	•	•		•		•		•		
	u				•	•	•	•		•		•		•		
	e						•	•		•		•		•		
	a								•	•		•		•		
	o										•	•		•		
2. Recognize the vowel sound /y/ for *y*, as in *lily*				•		•	•		•	•	•	•		•		
3. Recognize the sound /er/ for *er*		•	•	•		•		•				•	•	•		
4. Recognize the sound /er/ for *ir, ur*												•	•	•		
5. Recognize the sound /ar/ for *ar*														•	•	
6. Recognize the sound for these consonant digraphs:	unvoiced *th*, as in *with*		•			•				•			•			
	voiced *th*, as in *that*					•		•	•			•		•		
	wh, as in *what*			•										•		•
	ng, as in *ring*	•	•	•										•		
7. Recognize that a double consonant stands for one sound		•	•	•	•	•	•	•	•	•	•	•				
8. Recognize that *ck* stands for one sound: /k/					•	•			•		•		•			
9. Recognize these beginning consonant blends:	*br*, as in *bring*		•			•		•						•	•	
	dr, as in *drop*										•			•	•	
	fr, as in *from*					•	•	•						•		
	gr, as in *grass*									•				•		
	pr, as in *pretty*				•	•		•						•	•	
	tr, as in *truck*					•		•						•		
	bl, as in *black*								•					•	•	
	cl, as in *clock*										•			•		
	gl, as in *glass*									•				•		
	pl, as in *plan*															•
	sk, as in *skirt*											•		•	•	
	sl, as in *slim*													•		
	sm, as in *Smith*									•				•	•	
	st, as in *stop*					•				•		•	•	•		
	tw, as in *twelve*						•							•	•	
10. Recognize these ending consonant blends:	*nk*, as in *think*					•								•		
	nt, as in *hunt*							•						•		
	nd, as in *send*							•						•		
	nch, as in *lunch*										•			•		
	sk, as in *ask*														•	
	st, as in *just*															•
	ft, as in *left*															•
11. Recognize rhyming words								•	•	•	•		•			

Word recognition skills	Lesson	1	2	3	4	5	6	7	8	9	10	11	12	13	14	15
1. Recognize words by blending sounds		•	•	•	•	•	•	•	•	•	•	•	•	•	•	•
2. Recognize same words by sight in context		•	•	•	•	•	•	•	•	•	•	•	•	•	•	•
3. Recognize variants of root words																
— with noun endings:	*-s*	•				•	•					•				
	-'s	•	•			•						•	•			
	-s'		•			•								•	•	
— with verb endings:	*-s*						•	•				•	•			
	-ing		•	•	•					•		•				•
	-ed											•	•	•	•	•
— with adjective and noun ending *-er*													•			
— with noun or verb ending *-es*															•	•
4. Recognize root words in words with endings				•	•	•		•		•		•			•	•

Comprehension skills Lesson	1	2	3	4	5	6	7	8	9	10	11	12	13	14	15
1. Recognize a paragraph	•	•	•	•	•	•	•	•					•		
2. Read paragraph silently to answer questions about main idea	•	•	•	•	•	•		•							
3. Read story silently to answer questions about main idea										•	•	•		•	•
4. Scan story to find which paragraph tells certain main idea				•						•	•	•	•		
5. Scan story to locate specific details												•		•	•
6. State the main idea of a paragraph							•	•							
7. State the main idea of a story								•							
8. Summarize a story in own words				•	•	•		•	•		•	•	•		•
9. Recall sequence of events in a story					•					•		•	•		
10. Interpret facts and draw inferences	•	•	•	•	•	•	•	•	•	•	•	•		•	
11. Apply topics in story to everyday life	•	•	•	•	•	•	•	•	•	•	•	•			
12. Recognize direct quotations				•	•	•	•						•		
13. Identify speaker				•	•	•	•						•		
14. Observe punctuation as a key to sentence meaning: period				•			•	•		•					
comma				•			•	•		•					
quotation marks				•	•	•	•	•		•			•		
exclamation point				•			•	•					•		
question mark						•	•			•			•		
15. Read orally with expression							•		•		•	•	•		
16. Use a table of contents														•	•
17. Answer written Yes/No questions about a story														•	
18. Choose right word to complete a sentence about a story															•

Writing and spelling skills Lesson	1	2	3	4	5	6	7	8	9	10	11	12	13	14	15
1. Copy words	•	•	•		•										
2. Copy sentences	•	•	•	•	•										
3. Fill in missing letters in a word		•		•		•	•	•	•	•	•	•	•		
4. Fill in missing words in a sentence		•		•		•	•	•	•	•	•	•	•	•	•
5. Write regularly spelled words from dictation	•	•	•	•	•	•	•	•	•	•	•	•	•		
6. Write words with irregular spellings for some sounds	•	•	•	•	•	•	•	•	•	•	•	•	•		
7. Write sentences from dictation					•	•	•	•	•	•	•	•	•		
8. Write the question form of a written statement					•										
9. Write questions from dictation							•			•			•		
10. Form new words by adding these endings: -er													•		
-ed														•	
-s														•	
-es														•	
-ing															•
11. Recognize when to double the final consonant:															
— before adding -ing				•			•								•
— before adding -ed															•
12. Recognize how to add endings to words ending in e:															
— drop final silent e before -ing							•		•						•
— add r rather than -er to word ending in e												•			
— add -d rather than -ed to word ending in e															•
13. Recognize when to use c, k, or ck for the sound /k/:															
— k before e or i		•										•			
— c before a, o, u, or consonant		•			•		•			•	•	•			
— at end of word, ck after short vowel sound		•		•	•		•			•		•			
— at end of word, k after consonant					•							•			
14. Place address and return address correctly on envelope							•								

Lesson Notes Overview

Respellings

To help students sound out new words, some words are respelled, beginning in level 2. The policies for respelling are as follows:

1. The student should be able to pronounce the word for himself. This means that the respelling must contain only spelling patterns previously taught or being taught at this point.

2. The respelling should look as much like the actual spelling as possible.

The word is respelled only once. After that, the student will need to recognize it spelled correctly. Therefore, the respelling should give him the help he needs but not change the word so much that he won't recognize the word the next time he sees it.

Only the part of the word that is irregular or contains a regular spelling pattern not yet taught is changed in the respelling. If the pattern is being taught at the time the word is introduced, then it is usually not respelled.

Example: In Lesson 1, the word *little* is respelled *littul*. The last part of the word is changed, as the student would not otherwise know how to pronounce it. But double *t* for the sound /t/ is not changed. The concept that a double consonant is sometimes used for a single consonant is presented in this lesson.

3. The respelling uses the regular spelling pattern that is most similar to the way the word is spelled, provided that the pattern has been taught.

Example: In Lesson 11, the word *father* is respelled *fother*. This involves only one letter change and is the most similar pattern.

4. If one regular spelling pattern is no more similar than another to the part that needs to be respelled, the one that is most frequently used is chosen.

Example: The word *doctor* is respelled *docter*. The spelling *er* is more frequently used for the sound /er/ than is *ur* or *ir*.

5. The schwa sound (vowel sound that often occurs in an unstressed syllable) is respelled with the letter *u* where needed.

The schwa sound is represented in various words by any of the vowel letters. Most dictionaries use a special symbol (ə) to show the pronunciation of the schwa sound. The short sound for *u* is close to that pronunciation. In *Laubach Way to Reading*, therefore, the letter *u* is used to avoid introduction of a new symbol.

The schwa sound is respelled only where most needed to avoid a wrong pronunciation. Words in which the schwa sound is represented by *a* are the most likely to be respelled.

Examples: *Curtains (curtunz), another (unuther).* Words such as *seventy*, *garden*, and *market* are not respelled.

Notes on Style

Slash marks. Slash marks around a letter or letters indicate the sound for which they stand. Thus, you say /b/ like the beginning consonant sound in *bird,* and /a/ like the beginning vowel sound in *apple*.

Italics. Letters in italics are read by their letter names, as *a, b, c*. Words in italics are example words from the lesson, or examples of words similar in sound or spelling to lesson words.

Brackets [] and parentheses (). Brackets are used to enclose the expected student response. Parentheses are used to enclose what the teacher is expected to do.

Abbreviations. Many of the instructions for teaching the lessons are given in dialogue form. To save space, the letter *T* indicates *Teacher,* and the letter *S* indicates *Student*.

Pronouns referring to *teacher* and *student*. Although the authors recognize that there are teachers and students of both sexes, they have chosen for the sake of brevity to use the pronoun *she* to refer to the teacher and *he* to refer to the student.

Lesson Notes for Book 2

LESSON 1
Book 2
Pages 6–9

OBJECTIVES

To help your student:

- recognize the vowel *i* and its associated sound /i/ as in the key word *in*.
- recognize the sound /er/ as in *sister* and the sound /ng/ as in *ring*.
- recognize that a double consonant is sometimes used to stand for a sound usually represented by a single consonant, such as *ss* in *Miss* and *tt* in *little*.
- identify familiar sound-symbol relationships in a word, and blend the sounds to pronounce the word.
- read the following new words:
  Chart words: *Miss, sister, big, little, ring, finger*
  Story words: *it, gift, getting, giving*
  Instructions: *Study*.
- read a story, using the new chart and story words.
- read a paragraph silently to find the answer to a specific question.
- review the use of the endings *-s* and *-'s*.
- study some words that are not written the way they sound.
- write the correct letter for each sound of a word that is spelled the way it sounds.

INTRODUCTION

T: Today you will begin book 2. In this book, you will have a lot of practice on the short vowel sounds that you learned in the first book. You will also learn a few new consonant sounds. This book will help you learn how to sound out new words for yourself.

Give book 2 to S. On the cover, point to and read the series title *Laubach Way to Reading*. Then turn to the title page.

T: On this page, you see the title and subtitle of the book. The subtitle tells what the book is about. (Point to *Short Vowel Sounds*.) This says *Short Vowel Sounds*. Please read it. [S: Short Vowel Sounds.]

T: Vowel letters sometimes stand for other sounds. But most of the new words in this book have the short vowel sounds that you learned in book 1.

I. Reading

CHART: Page 6

Title and key word

T: The title at the top tells the lesson number. Please read it. [S: Lesson 1.]

T: In the top left-hand corner is the vowel that this lesson is about. (Point to the large *i* at top left.) What is the name of the vowel? [S: *i*.] Good.

T: (Point to the word *in*.) Here is the key word for *i* that you had in the first book. Please read it. [S: in.] (Point to *i* under *in*.) What is the sound for *i* in the word *in*? [S: /i/.] Very good.

T: In this lesson, you will have many words with the vowel sound /i/. We call /i/ the short sound for *i*. Later, you will learn its long sound.

Explanation of chart format

T: This chart has four columns. (Point to column 1.) The first column has a picture. (Point to column 2.) The second column has the word for the picture. (Point to column 3.) The third column has the word written in a special way to help you sound it out. (Point to column 4.) In the last column, you see the word again with its correct spelling as in column 2.

Line 1
Columns 1–2 (picture and word)

T: (Point to column 1.) The picture is here to give you a clue. You may not be able to tell exactly what the word is from the picture, but it will give you some idea. You may not need to look at the picture at all for help. You may be able to sound out the word.

T: Look at the first picture, and then look at the word next to it. (Point to the picture and then to the word *Miss*.) If you looked at just the picture, you might think it is a woman or girl. But when you look at the word and see what letter it begins with, you'll know it isn't *woman* or *girl*. What is the word? [S: Miss.] (If S. is not able to give the word, help him sound it out by referring to column 3.)

T: You had the words *Mr.* and *Mrs.* in book 1. *Miss* is also a title used with a name. That is why it is written with a capital *M*.

Columns 3–4 (word respelled and word printed again)

T: (Point to column 3.) Listen to the word *Miss*.
What letter stands for the first sound? [S: *M*.]
What letter stands for the vowel sound? [S: *i*.]
What letter stands for the last sound? [S: *s*.]

T: Usually, only one *s* is used for the sound /s/. But sometimes double *s* is used at the end of a word. In this column, the two *s*'s are put close together to show that they stand for one sound. Listen to the word again: *Miss*. How many sounds are in the word? [S: 3.]

T: Say each sound as I point to the letter or letters for the sound. [S: /m/.../i/.../s/.] In sounding out a word, try to hold on to one sound until you make the next. Slide the sounds together to make the word.

T: (Point to column 4.) Read the word again. [S: Miss.]

Line 4

T: Look at the next picture and word. (Point to the picture and the word *little*.) Compare this picture with the picture above; that will help you with the word. What is the word? [S: little.] (If necessary, help S. sound out the word by referring to column 3.)

T: (Point to column 3.) What is the first letter? [S: *l*.] What sound does *l* stand for? [S: /l/.] (Point to *i*.) What is the sound for this letter? [S: /i/.] What sound do the two *t*'s together stand for? [S: /t/.]

T: (Point to column 2.) Notice that *little* is written with an *e* at the end. But we don't hear this *e*. Instead, the ending sounds more like /u/ followed by /l/. If we wrote the word the way it sounds, we would write it like this. (Point to *ul* in column 3.) Say the sounds for these two letters. [S: /u/.../l/.]

T: Now say each sound in the word as I point to the letter or letters. [S: /l/.../i/.../t/.../u/.../l/.] Now blend the sounds quickly and say the whole word. [S: little.] Good.

T: (Point to column 4.) Read the word again. [S: little.]

Line 5

T: Look at the next picture and the word beside it. What is the word? [S: ring.] (If necessary, help S. sound out the word by referring to column 3.)

T: (Point to column 3.) Listen to the word *ring*. It ends with a new sound: /ng/. Say /ng/. [S: /ng/.] (Point to *ng*.) These letters stand for the sound /ng/. What are the letters? [S: *ng*.] What is the sound? [S: /ng/.] Read the word again. [S: ring.] We hear three sounds in *ring*, but we see four letters. Say each sound as I point to the letter or letters. [S: /r/.../i/.../ng/.] Now blend the sounds together and read the word. [S: ring.]

T: (Point to column 4.) Read the word again. [S: ring.]

Line 6

T: Look at the next picture and the word beside it. What is the word? [S: finger.] (If S. doesn't read the word, help him sound it out by referring to column 3.)

T: Look at column 3. Say each sound as I point to the letter. What is the beginning sound? [S: /f/.] What is the vowel sound? [S: /i/.] Next, you see the two letters for the new consonant sound that we had in *ring*. What is the sound? [S: /ng/.] We see another *g* because in the word *finger* we hear /g/ after /ng/. Say the sound for *g*. [S: /g/.] What is the ending sound? [S: /er/.] What two letters stand for /er/? [S: *er*.] Blend the sounds together and read the whole word. [S: finger.] Good.

T: (Point to column 4.) Read the word again. [S: finger.]

Review. Have S. read each word in the chart again as you point to it, going down the last column.

T: What vowel sound is in each of these words? [S: /i/.] What letter stands for the sound /i/? [S: *i*.]

Line 2

Columns 1–2 (picture and word)

T: Look at the next picture and the word beside it. (Point to the picture and then to the word *sister*.) Look at the first three letters. They will help you with the beginning of the word. At the end of the word, the letters *er* stand for a new sound: /er/. Now read the word. [S: sister.] (If necessary, help S. sound out the word, using column 3.)

Columns 3–4 (word respelled and word printed again)

T: Say each sound as I point to the letter or letters for the sound. Remember that the letters *er* stand for the sound /er/. [S: /s/.../i/.../s/.../t/.../er/.] Now blend the sounds quickly and say the whole word. [S: sister.] How many sounds are in the word? [S: 5.]

T: (Point to column 4.) Read the word again. [S: sister.]

Line 3

T: Look at the next picture and the word beside it. (Point to the picture and then to the word *big*.) Be sure to look at all the letters in the word. Think of the sound for each one. Then read the word. [S: big.]

T: Now look at the third column. Read the word to yourself, and notice how many sounds it has. How many? [S: 3.] Is there a letter for each sound? [S: Yes.] What is the vowel sound? [S: /i/.]

T: Look at the last column, and read the word again. [S: big.]

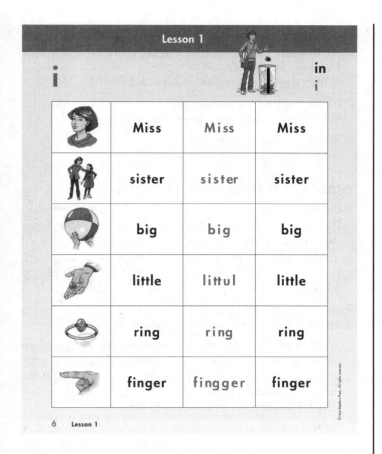

T: What is the ending sound in *sister* and *finger?* [S: /er/.]
   What two letters stand for the sound /er/? [S: *er.*]
   What is the ending sound of *ring?* [S: /ng/.]
   What other chart word has the sound /ng/? [S: finger.]
   What two letters stand for the sound /ng/? [S: *ng.*]

Have S. cover the picture column and read the words again as you point to them, going down the last column.

STORY: Page 7 (A Ring for Kim)

Ask S. to read the story title. Point to *ring* in the chart if he needs help with that word. Ask him if he remembers Kim's last name from book 1.

Story words

it, gift, getting, giving

Help S. sound out each new word. For *getting,* cover all but *get,* remind S. that he had this word in book 1, and ask him to read the word. Then have him read *getting.* Remind him that the two *t's* stand for one sound.

Paragraph 1

T: (Point to paragraph 1.) Read this paragraph to yourself, and find out who the girls are. [S. reads silently.] Who are the girls? [S: Miss Jill Hill and Miss Kim Hill.] Please read the paragraph aloud.

Paragraph 2

T: (Point to paragraph 2.) Read this paragraph to yourself and find out which one is the little sister. (Have S. tell the answer and then read the paragraph aloud.)

Paragraphs 3–7. Go through the rest of the story paragraph by paragraph. Have S. read each paragraph to find the answer to a specific question. If he has trouble with a word, refer him to the chart. Don't tell him a word before he has tried to sound it out. After he has read the paragraph silently, have him answer the question you asked. Then ask another question or two to check comprehension further. Finally, have S. read the paragraph aloud. Suggested questions for each paragraph are:

Par. 3. Where are the sisters?　　[S: In a gift shop.]
　　　　Whose shop is it?　　　　[S: Miss Oliver's.]

Par. 4. What are the sisters getting?　　[S: Gifts.]
　　　　Who is Kim getting a gift for?　[S: Mrs. Hill.]
　　　　Who is Jill getting a gift for?　[S: Kim.]

Par. 5. What gift does Jill give to Kim?　　[S: A ring.]

Par. 6. Where does Kim put the ring?
　　　　[S: On her little finger.]

Par. 7. What does Kim do?　　　[S: She thanks Jill.]

Oral reading. Have S. read the whole story aloud.

Reading between the lines. In this section, some questions will ask S. to relate facts in the story to each other or to draw inferences from clues in the story. Other questions will ask S. to draw upon his own experience and powers of reasoning to relate topics in the story to everyday life. The answers to such questions are neither stated nor implied in the stories themselves.

You should ask all of the questions that have to do with the story itself. You do *not* have to ask all of the other discussion questions, however. You may skip questions that would not be of interest or would be too sensitive. And you may substitute questions of your own.

Suggested answers will be given here only for the questions that relate to the story, but do allow some latitude here. The same thought may be expressed in different ways, and different answers are possible. If S. can make a reasonable case, his answer is acceptable.

Questions for this story are listed below:

1. The story tells us what gift Jill gets for Kim. But does it tell us what gift Kim gets for her mother? [No.]

2. Jill took Kim to the store with her to buy Kim a gift. Why would a person do this instead of keeping the gift a secret? [To make sure the person will like the gift. To make sure the gift will fit.]

3. If you had a choice, would you rather get a surprise gift, or would you rather help pick it out?

4. Before buying something for another person, why is it a good idea to find out the store's policy on returning things?

II. Skills Practice

T: Please close your book. We will do some practice exercises on listening for sounds and on adding some endings to words.

Note: In the listening exercises, the answers will be shown here only when it seems particularly helpful.

PRACTICE 1: Vowel Sound /i/

T: (Print the letter *i*.) Ask S. for the name and sound. Most of the new words in the story have the vowel sound /i/. I will say two words. Listen carefully.

T: Which word has the sound /i/:

big, on?	*it, to?*	*for, Hill?*
put, gift?	*giving, thanks?*	*has, is?*

PRACTICE 2: Beginning Sounds /f/, /l/, /m/, /r/

T: For this exercise, please open your book to page 6 and look at the chart. I will say two words that begin with the same sound as one word in the chart.

T: Which word in the chart begins with the same sound as these words:

leg, look? [S: little.]	*man, Mr.?* [S: Miss.]
fish, fill? [S: finger.]	*red, run?* [S: ring.]

PRACTICE 3: Ending Sounds /s, /er/, /ng/

T: Please point to the word *Miss* in the chart. I will say two words. Which word ends like *Miss: kiss, dish?*

T: Please point to the word *sister.* Which word ends like *sister: ring, mother?*

T: Please point to the word *ring.* Which word ends like *ring: run, sing?*

PRACTICE 4: Noun Endings -s and -'s

T: (Write *sister* on the board or on paper.) Read this word. [S: sister.] In the story, there are two sisters. What letter can we add to *sister* to mean more than one sister? [S: *s*.] That's right. (Add -*s* to *sister*.) Now read the word. [S: sisters.] Good. We can make some new words by adding -*s* to other words in the lesson.

Write *ring, gift, shop*. Have S. read each word. Then add -*s* to each word, and have him read the words with -*s*.

T: (Write *Kim's*.) We had this word in the story. Does it mean more than one Kim? [S: No.] We need another word after it to know what it means. (Write *finger* after *Kim's*.) Read these two words. [S: Kim's finger.] What does -*'s* mean? [S: The finger belongs to Kim.] Good.

T: We had some words with -*'s* in book 1. And there is another word with -*'s* in today's story. (Write *Miss Oliver's shop*.) Read this. [S: Miss Oliver's shop.]

Write the following phrases for S. to read: *Jill's sister, Kim's ring, Mrs. Hill's gift.*

III. Writing

CHECK HOMEWORK

Find out if S. has completed the book *In the Valley*. Talk about the stories he has read, and let him summarize them in his own words. If he hasn't finished the book, encourage him to do so.

WRITING LESSON: Page 8

T: Please open your book to page 8. (Point to the title.) What is the title of this page? [S: Writing Lesson.]

T: This page is divided into three parts. (Point to the word *Study*.) The first part is called *Study*. Read the word. [S: Study.] Often, there will be words in the lesson that are not written the way they sound. You will need to study these words before you can write them.

T: (Point to *Listen and write*.) In book 1, the lessons had a section with this title. What is it? [S: Listen and write.] After you study the words, I will say them for you to write. You will be able to write some of the words without much study because they are written the way they sound.

study
Study.

1. Miss   4. little

2. sister   5. ring

3. big   6. finger

Listen and write.

1. big   4. sister

2. Miss   5. little

3. ring   6. finger

Write.

Miss Hill

Mr. Hill

Mrs. Hill

8   Lesson 1

Write.

Miss

big

little

sister

This is a ring.

This is a finger.

Lesson 1   9

T: (Point to the third title, *Write.*) This says *Write.* Read it. [S: Write.] Here you will practice writing groups of words or sentences.

Study. Write *Miss* on the board or on paper. Or, have S. look at the chart.

T: Look at the word *Miss.* What kind of letter does it start with? [S: A capital.] What do you need to remember about the end of the word? [S: There are two *s*'s.] Close your eyes and picture the word in your mind. Say the letters to yourself. Now open your eyes and look at the word again. Find the word *Study* at the top of the Writing Lesson. Then write *Miss* by number 1. (Check to see that S. has written the word correctly.)

Follow the same procedure for each word in the chart, giving special attention to the *er, tt, ng,* and final *le* in *sister, little, ring,* and *finger.*

Listen and write. Ask S. to cover the "Study" part of the page. Then dictate these words for him to write:

1. big   4. sister
2. Miss   5. little
3. ring   6. finger

Have S. check his work by looking at the "Study" section. Ask him to correct any words he missed. It's a good idea to have him erase the whole word and write it again correctly.

Write. Have S. read the names. Call attention to the capital letters and the periods after the abbreviations *Mr.* and *Mrs.* Ask S. to copy each name.

HOMEWORK: Page 9.

T: Look at page 9. Here you have a page of homework as you did in book 1. (Point to the title.) Read the title. [S: Homework.] On the Homework page, you will practice writing some words and sentences.

Have S. read the words and sentences aloud. Call attention to the capital letter at the beginning of a sentence and the period at the end. Ask S. to write each word two times and each sentence one time at home. Suggest that he study the chart and read the story again at home. If he has not finished *In the Valley,* encourage him to do so.

CHECKING PROGRESS

Checkups for book 1. Go over the results of these checkups with S. if you have not already done so. Be sure that he understands anything that he did not do correctly.

Review of consonant sounds and letters. If the results of the checkups indicated that S. needed supplementary review lessons, it is assumed that you have given these before starting book 2.

But, if the results indicated that S. needs to review only a few skills, plan some practice exercises directly related to the lesson in book 2. For example, if S. needs practice on any consonants that are in the chart words for this lesson, plan additional exercises to help him master them. The workbook *Focus on Phonics 1* has exercises on the consonant sounds and letters which you may find useful. Let S. know what letters and sounds he needs to study the most. Keep a list of these, and check them off as he masters them.

Word recognition. Keep a list of old words that S. may not have been sure of when he was reading the story in this lesson. Make flash cards for these words. You can use these by themselves to practice recognition. Or, you can have S. put word cards together to make sentences.

MEETING INDIVIDUAL NEEDS

Some students may need to move at a slower pace and may need additional practice on certain skills. Or, you may be working with a student who can sight-read at a higher level than is in the skill book, but who is weak in phonics skills. The suggestions in this section will be especially helpful for both kinds of students. They may also be used when you have some extra time at the end of a lesson period.

Using flash cards. Make a flash card for each chart word in Lesson 1. In the top left-hand corner of each card, write the number 1. Then write the word. On the back side, write the word as it is written in column 3 of the chart, spacing out the letters for each sound and respelling when indicated.

Show S. the side of the card with the word written correctly. Turn the card over only if he needs help in sounding out the word. If he studies these cards at home, tell him to look at the side with number 1 on it first.

Make a separate flash card for each word needed to make the following sentences:

This is Kim's finger.	It is a little ring.
This is Miss Jill Hill.	It is Miss Oliver's shop.

Mix up the word cards for one sentence. Dictate the sentence, and have S. arrange the words in the right order. Do this for each sentence.

Using *More Stories 2*. The reader *More Stories 2* contains three stories correlated to the new words in each lesson of book 2. If S. needs extra reading practice, you may help him read some of these stories in class. If S. is able to read independently, he may enjoy and profit from reading these stories at home. You may want to wait until the end of Lesson 2 to introduce this book, however.

Using *Focus on Phonics*. The workbook *Focus on Phonics 2* uses a word-family approach (rhyming words) to help students learn many new short vowel words. It should be used only under your direction, with the help of the teacher's edition. This workbook is correlated to book 2. The numbered practices in the workbook may be used—at the earliest—following the skill book lesson of the same number. For example, Practices 1A–1C may be used after Lesson 1. But, if you use this workbook, you may want to complete all of the skill book lessons on a particular vowel sound before you use any of the workbook practices for that sound. Or, you may think that it would be better for your student to complete book 2 first and use *Focus on Phonics 2* afterward.

More Stories 2 will reinforce the vocabulary the student learns in each lesson of book 2. *Focus on Phonics 2* will help him transfer the phonics skills he learns in the skill book to many other new words. Keep these different purposes in mind when you select supplementary materials for your student.

Using *Workbook 2*. Although this workbook was developed for ESL students in the *Laubach Way to English* program, it can be helpful for native speakers of English, too. Besides providing an opportunity to review the book 2 words in a variety of contexts, the workbook gives practice with prepositions, pronouns, verb forms, making sentences, and answering questions. Many lessons contain a cloze exercise based on the story in the skill book lesson. In a cloze exercise, every 5th, 6th, 7th, 8th, or 9th word in the reading passage is left blank for the student to fill in. (The answer may be any appropriate word, not just the same word that was used in the story.) Cloze exercises integrate word recognition skills with the skills of using context and grammatical clues in the reading material.

Using *Puzzles 1 and 2*. New words are reviewed in one crossword puzzle for each lesson or two puzzles when the lesson has two charts and stories.

Using other supplements for reading practice. As the student progresses through book 2, he will benefit from actual reading in addition to practice in skills. Consult the inside front cover of this manual for suggested titles. You may want to read a passage to your student first, then read it aloud together with him one or more times, and let him read it aloud by himself until he is comfortable with it.

Be sensitive to the amount and the timing of any extra material you give your student to be sure that it is appropriate for him. Don't hold him back unnecessarily in order to cover all of the supplementary material suggested here. Don't give him so much new material that he becomes confused. And don't overburden him with so much extra practice that he becomes discouraged and loses a sense of progress.

OBJECTIVES

To help your student:

- read additional words with the vowel sound /i/.
- recognize the sound /wh/ as in *whistle*.
- identify the consonant blend /br/ as in *bringing*.
- review the sound /ng/ as in *ring* and the sound /er/ as in *sister*.
- read the following new words:
  Chart words: *kitchen, whistle, sitting, singing, bringing, dinner*
  Story words: *with, Hills'*
  Instructions: *Fill in the letters. Fill in the words.*
- read a story, using the new chart and story words.
- read a paragraph silently to find the answer to a specific question.
- read some variants of known words formed by adding or dropping the ending -*ing*.
- identify the ending -*s'* as in *the Hills' dinner*.
- write the new chart and story words.

INTRODUCTION

T: Many words have the short sound for *i*. In this lesson, you will read some more words with this sound.

I. Reading

CHART: Page 10

Title and key word. Have S. read the title *Lesson 2*.

T: Please point to the vowel in the top left-hand corner. What is the name of the vowel? [S: *i*.] What is the short sound for *i*? [S: /i/.]

T: (Point to *in*.) What is the key word? [S: in.]
(Point to *i*.) What sound does *in* begin with? [S: /i/.]

Line 1

T: Look at the first picture and the word next to it. (Point to them.) If you need help in sounding out the word, look at the third column. (Point to column 3.) What is the word? [S: kitchen.]

T: (Point to column 3)
Say each sound as I point to the letter.
[S: /k/.../i/.../ch/.../e/.../n/.]
What is the word? [S: kitchen.] Good.

Note: In an unstressed syllable, the sound for *e* is more like /u/ than /e/. The difference is slight, and S. will probably not notice. Don't mention it unless he asks.

T: (Point back to *kitchen* in column 2.) Notice that *kitchen* is written with a *t* in front of *ch*, but we do not hear a separate sound for the *t*. Listen to the word and tell how many sounds you hear: *kitchen*. [S: Five.] What is the sound for *ch*? [S: /ch/.]

T: (Point to column 4.) Read the word again. [S: kitchen.]

Line 2

T: (Point to column 1.) Look at the picture and the word next to it. You can probably tell what the word is from the picture. Read the word. [S: whistle.]

T: Listen to the word *whistle*. *Whistle* begins with the sound /wh/. This is a new sound. It is almost like the sound at the beginning of *woman*, but it has more breath to it. You let out a puff of air as you say the sound /wh/. Say *whistle*. [S: whistle.] Now say /wh/. [S: /wh/.] (Point to *wh* in *whistle*.) These two letters together stand for the sound /wh/. What are they? [S: *wh*.] What is the sound? [S: /wh/.]

Note: If S. doesn't make any distinction between /wh/ and /w/, don't emphasize the sound. Explain that some people say the sound for *wh* with more breath than for *w*, but other people do not. Either way is correct.

T: (Point to the *t* in *whistle*, and then point to column 3.) Notice that we don't hear a sound for the *t* in *whistle*. We say that the *t* is silent.

T: (Point to the *le* in *whistle*.) *Whistle* ends with the same sound as *little*. Remember that *le* at the end of a word sounds like /ul/. (Point to *ul* in column 3.)

T: (Point to column 3.) Say the sound as I point to each letter or letters. [S: /wh/.../i/.../s/.../u/.../l/.] Blend the sounds together and read the whole word. [S: whistle.]

T: (Point to column 4.) Read the word again. [S: whistle.]

Line 3

T: Look at the next picture and word. You can't tell from the picture exactly what the woman is doing. But you will be able to sound out the word. Look at column 3 if you need help in sounding it out.

T: (Point to column 2.) What is the word? [S: sitting.] (Point to column 3.) Say each sound as I point to the letter or letters. [S: /s/.../i/.../t/.../i/.../ng/.] Read the whole word. [S: sitting.]

T: How many sounds do you hear in the word? [S: Five.]
What is the vowel sound? [S: /i/.]
How many times do you hear /i/? [S: Twice.]
What sound does double *t* stand for? [S: /t/.]
What letters stand for the sound /ng/? [S: *ng*.]

T: (Point to column 4.) Read the word again. [S: sitting.]

Line 4

T: Look at the next picture and word. Read the word. [S: singing.]

T: (Point to column 3.) Say each sound as I point to the letter or letters. [S: /s/.../i/.../ng/.../i/.../ng/.] Read the whole word. [S: singing.]

T: How many sounds do you hear in the word? [S: Five.] How many times do you hear the vowel sound /i/? [S: Two.] How many times do you hear the sound /ng/? [S: Two.] What letters stand for the sound /ng/? [S: *ng.*]

T: (Point to column 4.) Read the word again. [S: singing.]

Line 5

T: Look at the next picture and word. You can't tell from the picture exactly what the man is doing. But you can sound out the word. Look at column 3 if you need help in sounding it out.

T: (Point to column 2.) What is the word? [S: bringing.] (Point to column 3.) Say each sound as I point to the letter or letters. [S: /b/.../r/.../i/.../ng/.../i/.../ng/.] Read the whole word. [S: bringing.]

T: How many times do you hear the sound /ng/? [S: Two.] What letters stand for the sound /ng/? [S: *ng.*] How many times do you hear the vowel sound /i/? [S: Two.]

T: (Point to *br.*) What two consonants do you see at the beginning of *bringing*? [S: *br.*] If you listen carefully, you can hear the sound for each of these consonants as you say the word. But the first consonant flows into the

second sound until it is almost one sound. We call this a *consonant blend.* Say these two consonant sounds quickly, blending them together. [S: /br/.] Now say the whole word. [S: bringing.]

T: (Point to column 4.) Read the word again. [S: bringing.]

Line 6

T: Look at the last picture and the word next to it. What is the word? [S: dinner.]

T: Look at column 3, and say each sound as I point to the letter or letters. [S: /d/.../i/.../n/.../er/.] Read the whole word. [S: dinner.]

T: How many sounds do you hear in *dinner*? [S: Four.] What is the last sound? [S: /er/.] What letters stand for the sound /er/ in *dinner*? [S: *er.*] What double consonant do you see in the word? [S: *n.*]

T: (Point to column 4.) Read the word again. [S: dinner.]

Review. Have S. read each word again, going down the last column of the chart. Then ask him to read the following:

1. The words that have the sound /ng/ as in *ring.*
2. The word that ends with the sound /er/ as in *sister.*
3. The word that begins with the sound /wh/ as in *what.*
4. The words that have double consonants.
5. The word that starts with the consonant blend *br.*

Cover the pictures, and have S. read all of the words again.

STORY: Page 11 (The Hills' Dinner)

Have S. read the story title. Help him sound out the new word *with*. Have S. read the new word *Hills'* (a variant of an old word), and tell him that he will learn about the ending *-s'* later in this lesson.

Directed silent reading. Follow these steps to teach each paragraph of the story:

1. Have S. read the paragraph silently to find the answer to a specific question. (If he has difficulty with a word, refer him to the chart. Do not tell him a word before he has tried to sound it out.)
2. Have S. answer the question you asked.
3. Ask another comprehension question or two.
4. Have S. read the paragraph aloud.

Suggested questions for each paragraph are:

Par. 1. Where is Mrs. Hill?   [S: In the kitchen.]
Who is with her?   [S: Jill.]
Is the kitchen big?   [S: Yes.]

Par. 2. Who is sitting in the kitchen? [S: Ed and Kim.]
Who is Ed's little sister?   [S: Kim.]

Par. 3. What is Ed doing?   [S: Whistling.]
What does he have? [S: A little whistle.]

Par. 4. What is Mrs. Hill doing?   [S: Singing.]
Who is she singing with?   [S: Kim and Jill.]

Par. 5. Why is Mr. Hill bringing a fish?
[S: He is bringing it for dinner.]
Is it a little fish?   [S: No, it's big.]

Par. 6. What do Jill and Ed bring?
[S: Jill brings a pan. Ed brings a dish.]

Par. 7. What are the Hills doing? [S: Sitting at dinner.]
What kind of dinner is it?   [S: A fish dinner.]
Whose dinner is it?   [S: The Hills'.]

Oral reading. Have S. read the whole story aloud.

Reading between the lines. Ask all of the questions that relate directly to the story. Select the general discussion questions that you think would be of most interest to S.

1. Where does this story take place? [In the Hills' kitchen.]
2. About what time of day does this story take place—morning, noon, or late afternoon? (If the word *dinner* is commonly used to refer to the noon meal in your area, tell S. that in other parts of the country, the evening meal is called dinner.)
3. When the story begins, which members of the Hill family are at home? [Mrs. Hill, Ed, Jill, Kim.] Who comes in later? [Mr. Hill.]
4. Did the Hill children do anything to help get dinner ready? [Yes.] Did they do this on their own, or did their parents have to tell them? [On their own.] Are children always as helpful as Jill and Ed seem to be?
5. Did the Hills seem to be in a good mood before dinner? [Yes.] What in the story shows that? [Singing, helping.] Is it important to be cheerful at meals. Why or why not?

6. The Hills ate their dinner together. Why do some families make a special effort to eat at least one meal a day together? Why is it sometimes hard for a family to get together for meals? Should children always eat with adults? Why or why not?

II. Skills Practice

T: Please close your book. We will have some practice exercises on some sounds and endings in this lesson.

PRACTICE 1: Beginning Sound /wh/

Note: The letters *wh* form a consonant digraph. A consonant digraph is a combination of two consonant letters that stand for a single sound. In book 1, S. learned the consonant digraphs *ch, sh, th.*

The first part of this exercise will help S. distinguish the digraph *wh* from other digraphs.

T: Listen to this word and tell me the beginning sound: *whistle.* [S: /wh/.] What two letters stand for the sound /wh/ as in *whistle*? [S: wh.] (Write *wh* on the board or on paper.)

T: I will say two words.
Which word begins with /wh/ as in *whistle:*
where, there?   when, chin?   that, what?

The next part of this exercise will help S. hear the difference between the sounds /wh/ and /w/. Omit this part if S. makes no distinction between these sounds in his speech. You may also skip this part if you're not sure that *you* can make a distinction between the sounds.

T: I will say two words. One word will begin with the sound /wh/ as in *whistle.* The other word will begin with the sound /w/ as in *woman.* Listen carefully.

T: Which word begins like *whistle:*
will, wheel? wine, whine? where, wear? whip, weep?

PRACTICE 2: Ending Sounds /sh/ and /th/

T: What sound does this word end with: *fish*? [S: /sh/.]
What two letters stand for the sound /sh/? [S: sh.]
(Write *sh* on the board or on paper.)

T: Which word ends with /sh/ as in *fish:*
dish, says? Miss, mash? hash, lunch? catch, cash?

T: Tell me the ending sound of this word: *with.* [S: /th/.]
What two letters stand for the sound /th/? [S: th.]
(Write *th* on the board or on paper.)

T: Which word ends with /th/ as in *with:*
bat, bath? Beth, Bess? boat, both? month, must?

PRACTICE 3: Beginning Consonant Blend *br*

Note: The letters *br* form a consonant blend. In a consonant blend, two or three consonants are sounded together, but each of these sounds is still heard distinctly. In this way, a blend is different from a digraph, which has just one sound.

T: Listen to this word, and tell me what two consonant sounds you hear at the beginning: *bring*. [S: /br/.] Good. We hear the sound for both *b* and *r*, but they are blended together. (Write *br*.) Remember, we call this a consonant blend.

T: Which word begins with the consonant blend *br*:
brother, Bob?   ride, bride?   brag, rag?
bridge, badge?   red, bread?   round, brown?

PRACTICE 4: Finding Root Word by Subtracting *-ing*

Write the words *singing, bringing, sitting* on the board, one under the other. Remind S. that he had these words in the story, and have him read them.

T: What three letters does each of these words end with? [S: *-ing*.] I'll draw a line under that part of each word. (Underline the *-ing* in each word.) We call this part the *-ing* ending. We can make new words from these words by leaving off the *-ing* ending.

T: Leave *-ing* off *singing*. What is the word? [S: sing.] (Write *sing* next to *singing*.)

Continue in the same way with the other words.

T: In our last lesson, we had two other words that end with *-ing: getting* and *giving*. (Write these words.)

T: Leave *-ing* off *getting*. What is the word? [S: get.] (Write *get* next to *getting*.)

Continue in the same way with *giving/give*.

PRACTICE 5: Recognizing the Ending *-s'*

Write *the Hills' dinner* and have S. read it.

T: Whose dinner is it? [S: The Hills'.]
Does it belong to just one of them? [S: No.]

T: We show that it belongs to all of them by putting the apostrophe after the *-s*. (Point to apostrophe.) But, if we wanted to say *Mr. Hill's dinner*, we would write it this way. (Write *Mr. Hill's dinner*.) Where is the apostrophe? [S: Before the *-s*.] That is to show that the dinner belongs to just one person, Mr. Hill.

Write the following phrases, and have S. read them. Ask him to tell what the *-'s* or *-s'* ending means in each case.

the girl's ring   the boy's pup   Ed Hill's whistle
the girls' rings   the boys' pups   the Hills' kitchen

III. Writing

CHECK HOMEWORK: Page 9

Check this page with S. If he didn't write the words at home, give him a few minutes to do so in class. Also, find out if he has completed *In the Valley* or has any questions about it.

CHECKUP: Page 12

Title and new words. Ask S. to open his book to page 12.

T: This is a Checkup on the new words in Lesson 1. It is something like the Checkups in your first book. (Point to the title.) Read the title. [S: Checkup.]

T: There are three new words in the directions on this page. (Point to *fill, letters (letterz), words (werdz)* at top right.) You can sound out these words.

Point to each word, and have S. sound it out, giving help if needed. For *letters* and *words*, explain that next to the word, in parentheses, the word is written the way it sounds. Finally, have S. read all three words.

Fill in the letters. Have S. read the directions. Explain that in each word, one or two letters are missing. The picture and the beginning letters will help him know what the word is. Tell him to say each word to himself and write the missing letters. To be sure he understands what to do, have him say the first word aloud [*big*] and tell you what the missing letter is [*i*].

Let S. work as independently as he can. If he hesitates on a word, ask him to say it aloud. If he doesn't know what the word should be, say it for him and let him fill in the missing letters.

After he finishes, have him read each word and tell what letter or letters he filled in. Check to see that he wrote the letters correctly. Have him correct any errors.

Fill in the words. Have S. read the directions.

T: One word is missing in each of these sentences. Read the sentence, and think of the missing word. It will be one of the words from the exercise that you have just done. Write the correct word in the blank.

Have S. read the first sentence aloud, saying the missing word before he writes it. Then let him complete the other sentences. After he finishes, have him read each sentence aloud. Check to see that he wrote the missing word correctly. Have him correct any errors.

WRITING LESSON: Page 13

Study. Have S. read the title of the page, *Writing Lesson*, and the direction word for the first section, *Study*.

T: In the chart, there are two words that are not written just as they sound. You will need to study them the most before you write them. And there are some points to remember about the other words. Please turn back to the chart on page 10.

The word *kitchen*

T: (Point to *kitchen* in column 2 of the chart.) Read the word. [S: kitchen.] What letter stands for the sound /k/ in *kitchen*? [S: *k*.] What letter stands for the sound /i/? [S: *i*.] When the sound /k/ is followed by *i*, we almost always use a *k* instead of a *c*.

T: What letter comes after *i*? [S: *t*.] You don't hear a sound for *t*. So you must remember to write *t* after *i*. What letters stand for the sound /ch/? [S: *ch*.]

20   Lesson 2

T: What vowel letter comes after *ch*? [S: *e.*] It sounds more like /u/ when we say it, but you will remember to write *e*. What is the last sound in *kitchen*? [S: /n/.] What letter stands for the sound? [S: *n.*]

T: Listen to the first part of the word: /kich/. Say the letters for this part. [S: *k—i—t—c—h.*]

T: Listen to the last part of the word: /un/. Say the letters for this part. [S: *e—n.*]

T: Look at the word *kitchen* again. Say it. [S: kitchen.] Close your eyes and try to see the word in your mind. Say the letters out loud. [S: *k—i—t—c—h—e—n.*]

T: Turn to page 13. Write the word *kitchen* by number 1. (Have S. check his work by looking back at the chart.)

The word *whistle*

T: (Point to *whistle* in column 2 of the chart.) Read the word. [S: whistle.] What two letters stand for the sound /wh/ in *whistle*? [S: *wh.*] What letter stands for the sound /i/? [S: *i.*] What letter stands for the sound /s/? [S: *s.*]

T: (Point to *t.*) Remember that there is a silent letter in *whistle*. What is it? [S: *t.*]

T: Then you hear /ul/, but this is written *le* at the end of this word.

T: Listen to the first part of the word: /whis/. Say the letters for this part. [S: *w—h—i—s.*]

T: What is the silent letter you must remember? [S: *t.*] Say the letters for the last part of the word that sounds like /ul/. [S: *l—e.*]

T: Look at the whole word again. Say it. [S: whistle.] Close your eyes and see it in your mind. Spell it out loud. [S: *w—h—i—s—t—l—e.*]

T: Turn to page 13, and write *whistle* by number 2. Then look back at the chart to see if you wrote it correctly.

The remaining words. Have S. study the other words in the same way. Give special attention to the *tt, nn, er, br* blend, *ng,* and *-ing* ending in *sitting, singing, bringing, dinner.*

These are the main steps in studying a word:

1. Look at the word.
2. Say the word.
3. Note the part that is written the way it sounds.
4. Note the part that is *not* written as it sounds.
5. Note any special points to remember.
6. Say the word again.
7. Say the letters in sequence. (If the word has two syllables, you may have S. say the letters for each part of the word at this point.)
8. Look at the word again.
9. Close your eyes, and see the word in your mind.
10. Spell the word aloud.
11. Write the word without looking at a model.
12. Check to see if you are right.

Listen and write. Have S. read the directions. Have S. cover the "Study" section, and dictate these words for him to write:

1. dinner
2. whistle
3. kitchen
4. sitting
5. bringing
6. with

S. should be able to write the story word *with* by listening to the sounds. Have him check his work by looking at the chart and the story words. If he made any mistakes, have him erase and write the whole word correctly.

Write. Have S. read the direction word. Have him read the name *Ed Hill.* Call attention to the capitals. Have him copy the name. Then have S. read the two sentences. Call attention to the capitals and periods. Ask S. to copy the sentences.

HOMEWORK: Pages 14–15

Page 14. Have S. read *Homework* and the instruction *Write.* Have him read the sentences. Tell him to write each sentence once. Remind him to use a capital at the beginning of the sentence and a period at the end.

Page 15. Have S. read *Homework* and the two instructions, *Fill in the letters* and *Fill in the words.* Be sure he understands what to do in each part. Tell him to try to write the answers without looking back at the chart.

Also, ask S. to study the chart and read the story again at home, and to study any words he wasn't sure of in the "Listen and write" exercise.

CHECKING PROGRESS

Keep notes on the progress S. is making. Does he connect the sound /i/ with the letter *i*? Does he recognize the new sounds and letters? Is his ability to sound out words improving? Is he learning how to study words in order to spell them? List any sounds and letters and any words in the story that S. is not sure of, and give extra practice on them. Note his progress in reading silently and his comprehension of what he reads.

MEETING INDIVIDUAL NEEDS

Make flash cards for the chart words in this lesson as suggested for Lesson 1. Also, make flash cards for the following: *er, ng, wh, br, ing.* Say a word such as *dinner,* and have S. find the card for the ending sound. Or, show a card such as *wh* or *br,* and ask him to say a word that begins with those letters.

Make flash cards for the words in a sentence, such as: *It is a big kitchen.* Mix up the cards, say the sentence, and have S. put the cards in order.

Practices 2A–2D of *Focus on Phonics 2* may be used after Lesson 2. Or, you may prefer to save all the short *i* practices to use as a review after Lesson 3.

In *More Stories 2,* the stories for Lesson 1 may be read in class or suggested for reading at home.

fill, letters (letterz), words (werdz)

Fill in the letters.

 b i g

 fing e r

 li t tle

 M i ss

 sist e r

 ri n g

Fill in the words.

1. This is __Miss__ Jill Hill.

2. Jill is Kim's big __sister__.

3. The gift is a __ring__.

4. It is a __little__ ring.

5. The ring is on Kim's __finger__.

Study.

1. kitchen   4. singing

2. whistle   5. bringing

3. sitting   6. dinner

Listen and write.

1. dinner   4. sitting

2. whistle   5. bringing

3. kitchen   6. with

Write.

Ed Hill

It is a kitchen.

Jill is singing.

Write.

It is a big kitchen.

I am sitting with Mrs. Hill.

He is bringing a fish.

She is singing with Kim.

Fill in the letters.

 kitchen

 whistle

 si t ting

si n ging

Fill in the words.

1. Jill is in the __kitchen__.

2. Ed is sitting with __Kim__.

3. Ed is sitting with his little __sister__.

4. Mr. Hill is __bringing__ a fish.

5. This is a fish __dinner__.

OBJECTIVES

To help your student:

- identify the vowel *i* and its associated short sound.
- recognize *y* as a vowel at the end of a word and associate its vowel sound /y/ as in *city*.
- review the sound /ng/ as in *King*.
- read the following new words:
  Chart words: *lily, city, windy, Kitty, Jimmy, building, picture*
  Story words: *Ms., King, Fisher, pretty.*
- read a story, using the new chart and story words.
- read a paragraph silently to find the answer to a specific question.
- identify the consonant blend *pr* as in *pretty*.
- recognize known words, including those ending in *e*, when the ending *-ing* is added or subtracted.
- study some words that are not written the way they sound.
- write the new chart and story words.

INTRODUCTION

T: In this lesson you will read some more words with the short vowel sound for *i*. And you will read some words in which the letter *y* stands for a vowel sound.

Note: The sound for y at the end of an unstressed syllable is somewhere between the short *i* sound /i/ and the long *e* sound /ē/. Have S. pronounce words ending in *y* as he would naturally say them. But refer to the sound as the vowel sound for *y*, not the long sound for *e*.

I. Reading

CHART: Page 16

Title and key word. Have S. read the title *Lesson 3*.

T: Look at the letter in the top left-hand corner. What is the name of this letter? [S: *y*]

T: In book 1, you learned the sound for *y* as in *yell*. What is the sound? [S: /y/.] In the word *yell, y* is a consonant. (Write *yell* on the board.) Where is *y* in the word *yell*? [S: At the beginning.] When *y* is at the beginning of a word, it is a consonant. But, when *y* is at the end of a word, it is a vowel.

T: Look at the picture and key word. The word is *lily*. Read it. [S: lily.] Where does the letter *y* come in the word *lily*? [S: At the end.] So *y* has a vowel sound. Listen to the word again: *lily*. The ending sound is /y/. (Say /i/ or /ē/ according to your student's speech pattern.) Say /y/. [S: /y/.] The sound /y/ is one of the vowel sounds for *y*.

T: Read the word again. [S: lily.] What kind of sound does *y* have in *lily*? [S: A vowel sound.]

T: You will read some other words in the chart that have the vowel sound for *y*.

Line 1

T: Look at the first word and picture. The word is not written just the way it sounds. So, look at the next column and sound out the word. What letter does *c* sound like in this word? [S: *s*.] What is the first vowel in the word. [S: *i*.] What is the next letter? [S: *t*.] What is the last letter? [S: *y*.] What sound does it have? [S: /y/.] Blend the sounds together and say the word. [S: city.]

T: (Point to column 4.) Read the word again. [S: city.]

Line 2. Have S. sound out *windy*. Remind him that *y* has a vowel sound because it's at the end of the word. Ask him how many sounds [five] and how many letters [five] the word has. Have him read the word again in column 4.

Line 3. Have S. sound out *Kitty*. Ask him what kind of *k* the word begins with [capital], and point out that this is because *Kitty* is used here as a woman's name. Ask S. what double letter the word has and what two vowels are in the word. Have him read the word again in column 4.

Line 4. Tell S. that this word is a man's name, and have him sound out *Jimmy*. Ask him what double letter the word has. Then ask how many sounds [four] and how many letters [five] the word has. Have him read the word again in column 4.

Line 5

T: Look at the next picture and word. This word is not written just the way it sounds. So look at column 3 for help in sounding it out. Blend the sounds together and read the word. [S: building.]

T: Compare column 2 and column 3. Which letter is left out in column 3 because it's silent in *building?* [S: *u*.]

Have S. read the word again in column 4.

Line 6

T: Look at the last picture and word. Look at column 3 for help in sounding it out. Blend the sounds and say the word. [S: picture.]

T: Compare columns 2 and 3. The first part of the word, *pic,* sounds the way it is written. But the second part sounds different. (Point to *t* in column 2 and *ch* in column 3.) What sound do you say for t in this word? [S: /ch/.] (Point to *ure* in column 2 and *er* in column 3.) What sound do you say for the letters *ure*? [S: /er/.] Say the whole word. [S: picture.]

Have S. read the word again in column 4.

Review. Have S. read each word again, going down the last column of the chart. Then ask him to read the following:

1. The key word.
2. The other words that end with *y*.

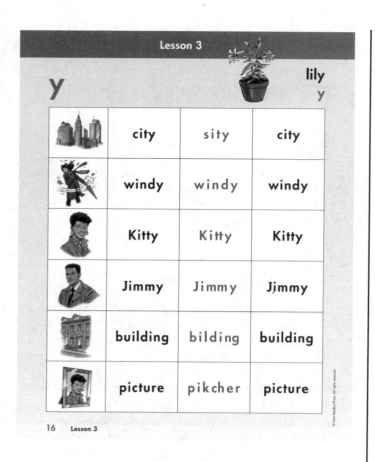

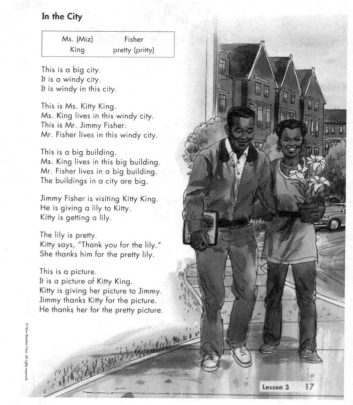

3. The words that have double letters.
4. The word that ends in *-ing*.

Cover the pictures, and have S. read all the words again.

STORY: Page 17 (In the City)

Have S. read the story title and the new story words. Tell him that *Ms.* is a title used with a woman's name, and have him sound it out by looking at how it is written in parentheses. Have him sound out *King, Fisher, pretty.*

Directed silent reading. Have S. read each paragraph silently to find the answer to a specific question and then give the answer. You may want to ask additional questions to check his comprehension. If he has trouble answering, have him read the paragraph aloud and pick out the part that answers the question.

From now on, the answers to suggested questions will be shown here only when it seems especially helpful.

Par. 1. What kind of city is it?

Par. 2. What are the names of the people in the story? Where do they live?

Par. 3. What kind of buildings are in a city? Do Kitty and Jimmy live in the same building? [No.] (Discuss the difference in meaning between *this big building* and *a big building*.

Par. 4. What is Kitty getting? Who is giving it to her?

Par. 5. What does Kitty do when Jimmy gives her the lily? Is the lily pretty?

Par. 6. What does Kitty give to Jimmy? What does Jimmy do when Kitty gives him the picture?

Oral reading. Have S. read the whole story aloud.

Word study

T: There are three words in the story that tell what something is like. One word is *big*. What are the other two? [S: *Windy* and *pretty*.] What things in the story are said to be pretty? [S: The lily and the picture.] What is described as big? [S: The city, the buildings.] What is described as windy? [S: The city.]

Ask S. to find each of the new story words in the story.

Reading between the lines. Discuss these questions.

1. Do you think Kitty lives in an apartment or a house? [Apartment.] Why do you think so? [The story says she lives in a big building, and it's in a city.]

2. Do you think that Kitty and Jimmy know each other fairly well? [Yes.] Why do you think so? [Because they're giving each other gifts.]

3. Ask S. to name the capital city and one or two other cities in his state. Talk about some of the biggest cities in the country. You may want to write the names of these cities for him or point them out on a map.

II. Skills Practice

T: Please close your book. We'll have some practice on the short sound for *i*, a new consonant blend, and the ending *-ing*.

PRACTICE 1: Vowel Sound /i/

T: In the first three lessons, you have had many words with the short sound for *i*. I'm going to say three words. Which words have the sound /i/ in them:

living, thank, Kitty?　　[S: living, Kitty.]
up, it, lily?　　　　　　[S: it, lily.]
him, visiting, Ed?　　　[S: him, visiting.]

PRACTICE 2: Beginning Consonant Blend *pr*

T: Listen to this word, and tell me what two consonant sounds you hear at the beginning: *pretty.* [S: /pr/.] Good. We hear the sounds for both *p* and *r*, but they are blended together. (Write *pr*.) This is another consonant blend.

T: Which word begins with the consonant blend *pr*:

print, pick?　　*ride, pride?*　　*problem, pocket?*
pet, press?　　*price, rice?*　　*penny, present?*

PRACTICE 3: Adding and Subtracting *-ing*

Write *building, visiting, getting, giving* in a column. Have S. read each word and tell what it would be without *-ing*. As he tells you, write the form without *-ing* by each word: *build, visit, get, give.*

Write *thank* and *live* in a column. Have S. read each word and tell what it would be with *-ing* added. As he tells you, write *thanking* by *thank* and *living* by *live*. Explain that when *-ing* is added to *live*, the *e* is dropped.

III. Writing

CHECK HOMEWORK: Pages 14–15

Check these pages with S. Allow time in class if he hasn't completed the work. Have him correct any errors.

WRITING LESSON: Page 18

Study. Have S. read the title of the page, *Writing Lesson,* and the direction word for the first part, *Study.*

T: In the chart, there are some words that are not written just the way they sound. Please look at the chart on page 16.

Note: As S. studies the words on the chart, be sure he looks at the correct spelling in column 2 and *not* at the respelling in column 3. It's a good idea to cover column 3.

The word *city*. Have S. find *city* on the chart.

T: What is the first sound in *city*? [S: /s/.] What letter is used for the sound /s/ in *city*? [S: *c*.] What is the last letter in *city*? [S: *y*.]

T: Look at the word *city* in column 2. Say the letters to yourself. Then close your eyes, and try to see the word *city* in your mind. Look back at *city* in column 2 to see if you were right. (Give S. time to do this.) Now turn to page 18, and write *city* by number 1. (Have S. check his work by looking back at the chart.)

The remaining words. Follow the same general procedure. For *Kitty*, remind S. that /k/ followed by *i* is written with *k* instead of *c*. Also, point out the capital *K* on the name, the *tt*, and the *y* at the end.

For *Jimmy*, point out the capital *J*, the *mm*, and the *y* at the end.

For *pretty*, write the word on the board. Point out the consonant blend *pr*, the letter *e* for the sound /i/, the *tt*, and the *y* at the end.

For *building*, point out the silent *u* and the *-ing* ending.

For *picture*, help S. study the second part by saying the letters *ture*, not by sounding them out.

Listen and write. Have S. read the directions. Have him cover the "Study" section, and dictate these words for him to write:

1. lily　　　　4. Kitty
2. windy　　　5. pretty
3. visiting　　6. city

Have S. check his work by finding the words in the chart and story (*visiting* is in paragraph 4). Have him correct any errors by erasing the whole word and writing it over.

Write. Have S. read the directions *Write* and the words. Call his attention to the capitals in the names. Then have him copy the whole section.

HOMEWORK: Page 19

Have S. read the title and everything on the page aloud. Ask him to tell which lines are sentences and how he knows they are sentences. Call attention to the period after the abbreviation *Ms*. Ask him to copy each line at home. Also, encourage him to review Lessons 1–3 by studying the charts and reading the stories at home.

CHECKING PROGRESS

Check your student's progress in these ways:

1. Use flash cards of the chart words in Lessons 1–3. Show S. a word. Give him time to sound it out. If he hesitates or says the word incorrectly, tell him the word, and put a check by it to show that he needs to study it more.

2. Use flash cards for the letters *wh, br, pr*. Have S. give the sound for each and say a word that begins with that sound. If he can't think of a word, say two words, one of which has the sound, and let him choose the right one.

Study.

1. city   4. pretty

2. Kitty   5. building

3. Jimmy   6. picture

Listen and write.

1. lily   4. Kitty

2. windy   5. pretty

3. visiting   6. city

Write.

Jimmy Fisher

Kitty King

a windy city

18   Lesson 3

Write.

Ms. King

Mr. Fisher

getting a lily

in the city

This is Jimmy Fisher.

He gives a lily to Kitty.

She thanks him.

Lesson 3   19

---

3. Use flash cards for the letters *ng* and *er*. Have S. give the sound for each and say a word that ends with that sound.

4. Dictate these sounds and ask S. to write the letter or letters for the sounds:

—/wh/ as in *whistle*
—/br/ as in *bring*
—/pr/ as in *pretty*
—/ng/ as in *ring*

—/er/ as in *sister*
—/i/ as in *Miss*
—/y/ as in the last sound of *lily*.

MEETING INDIVIDUAL NEEDS

If S. has kept up with most of the material covered in the first three lessons and did reasonably well in the exercises suggested above, let him go ahead with Lesson 4. But, if you think he would profit from a review lesson, plan one for next time. In addition to suggestions given in Lessons 1–2 for reinforcing skills, you may find the following exercises helpful.

1. If S. is having trouble distinguishing the sound /i/, make flash cards for some pairs of known words that are the same except for the vowel sound, as: *in/an, on/in, his/has, it/at, pick/pack.* Give S. one pair of cards at a time, such as *his/has.* Read a sentence such as *Ed has*

a gun, and have S. pick the word. Read two or three sentences for each pair.

2. Many of the new words are nouns or adjectives. Use these for a substitution exercise, choosing words S. needs to practice. Arrange word cards to form a simple sentence, as: *The ring is little.* Put noun cards that can be substituted for *ring* on the student's left. Put adjective cards that can be substituted for *little* on his right. Have S. read the sentence you arranged. Then say another sentence, changing *one* word. Have S. find the word card for it and substitute it in the sentence. Some examples of substitutions are:

The ring is *little.*
The ring is *big.*
The *city* is big.
The *building* is big.

In *More Stories 2*, the stories for Lesson 2 may be read in class or suggested for reading at home.

Practices 3A–3D in *Focus on Phonics 2:* Part A may be used after Lesson 3. Or, if you have saved all of the short *i* practices to use as a review, you may do them now. Another possibility is to save all of *Focus on Phonics 2:* Part A to use after completing book 2.

OBJECTIVES

To help your student:

- recognize the vowel *u* and its associated short sound /u/ as in the key word *up*.
- recognize the use of the letter *c* for the sound /k/ before the letter *u*, as in *cut*.
- recognize the use of the letters *ck* to stand for the sound /k/ after a short vowel.
- understand that a consonant after a short vowel sound is usually doubled before adding the *-ing* ending.
- observe the use of a comma to indicate a brief pause.
- read the following new words:
  Chart words: *gun, sun, son, duck, hunting, cut, cutting*
  Story words: *hit, mud, bring*.
- read a story, using the new chart and story words.
- read direct quotations.
- scan material to find main ideas.
- write the new chart and story words.

INTRODUCTION

T: You have read many words with the short sound for *i*. Today you will have a lesson about a different vowel.

I. Reading

CHART: Page 20

Title and key word. Have S. read the title *Lesson 4*.

T: Look at the letter in the top left-hand corner. What is the name of the letter? [S: *u*.]

T: (Point to *up*.) What is the key word? [S: up.]
(Point to *u*.) What sound does *up* begin with? [S: /u/.]
We call /u/ the short sound for *u*.
Later, you will learn its long sound.

Lines 1–6

T: In this lesson, there are many words with the vowel sound /u/. Most of the words are pronounced just the way they are written. Only one word is changed to help you read it. Study the chart, and read the words to yourself.

After S. has studied the chart silently, have him read each word aloud. Call attention to the following points:

1. The difference in meaning and spelling between *sun* and *son*.

2. The use of *ck* for the sound /k/ in *duck*. (Explain as in the following paragraph.)

T: You have had words that end with a double consonant after a short vowel sound, as in the words *Miss* and *Hill*. After a short vowel sound, instead of using a double *k* for /k/, we use *ck*. These two letters stand for one sound.

3. The use of *c* for the sound /k/ when it is followed by *u*, as in *cut*. Remind S. that *k* is used for /k/ when followed by *i*, as in *kitchen* and *Kitty*.

4. The *-ing* ending in *hunting*. Ask what the word would be without the ending.

5. The *-ing* ending in *cutting*. Call attention to the double *t* in *cutting*.

Review. Have S. read all of the words again, going down the last column of the chart.

STORY: Page 21 (Duck Hunting)

Have S. read the story title and the new story words: *hit, mud, bring* (a variant of the old word *bringing*).

Directed silent reading. Have S. read each paragraph silently to find the answer to a specific question. After he has answered that question, you may want to ask one or two other questions to check his comprehension.

Suggested questions for each paragraph are:

Par. 1. Who has a big gun? Which words tell whose gun it is? [Mr. Hill's.]

Par. 2. Who is hunting with Mr. Hill? Who is Ed? What are they hunting?

Par. 3. What are Mr. Hill and his son looking at? What time of day do you think it is? [Early morning.]

Par. 4. Who hits a duck? What does he yell?

Par. 5. Where is the duck? Who picks up the duck?

Par. 6. Who brings the duck to the tent? Who cuts up the duck?

Par. 7. What does Mr. Hill thank his son for?

Summarizing the story. Have S. read the whole story again to himself. Then ask him to tell in a few sentences what happened in the story. He might summarize the story as follows:

[Mr. Hill and his son are duck hunting. Ed hits a duck. It falls into the mud. Mr. Hill tells Ed to bring the duck to the tent and cut it up. Ed does that. Mr. Hill thanks his son.]

Scanning the story to find a main idea. Tell S. to look quickly down the page and find the paragraph you describe. When he has found it, have him read it aloud.

1. The paragraph that tells about the sun in the sky.
2. The paragraph that tells who is hunting.
3. The paragraph that tells what Ed yells.
   (In this paragraph, point to the comma, and remind S. that a comma tells us to pause briefly.)
4. The paragraph that tells who cuts up the duck.

Word study. Have S. find these words in the story:

1. The new story words *mud, hit, bring*.
2. The words that end with *-ing* (*hunting, looking, cutting*).
3. The word that ends like *duck* (*pick*).

Punctuation review. Have S. find each of these punctuation marks in the story: *period, comma, quotation marks, exclamation point*. Review what they mean.

Oral reading. Have S. read the part that Ed yells in paragraph 4. Remind him to observe the quotation marks and to read just the part between them. Then ask him to read the part that Mr. Hill yells in paragraphs 5, 6, 7.

Finally, have S. read the whole story aloud.

Reading between the lines. Discuss some of these questions.

1. What do you think of Mr. Hill as a father? What in the story helped you form your opinion?
2. If S. is very interested in hunting, you may want to spend some time discussing hunting in your area, hunting regulations, and the safe use of a gun.
3. If S. is not interested in hunting, ask what sport or recreation he does enjoy and why. What are some sports that families can take part in together, as Mr. Hill and his son did?

II. Skills Practice

T: Please close your book. We will have some exercises on the vowel sounds /u/ and /i/ and on the ending *-ing*.

PRACTICE 1: Vowel Sounds /u/ and /i/

T: Which word has the vowel sound /u/ as in *up:*

but, bit?   cut, cat?   hunt, hint?
hit, hut?   mad, mud?   him, hum?

T: We can often change a word into another word just by changing the vowel sound. Listen to each word I say. If you change /u/ to /i/, what is the word:

sun? [S: sin.]   *bug*? [S: big.]
but? [S: bit.]   *hut*? [S: hit.]

T: The vowel sound is very important. Unless we read it and say it clearly, we may not say the right word.

PRACTICE 2: Doubling the Final Consonant Before *-ing*
Recognizing root words

T: You have had several words to which the ending *-ing* has been added. We call the word without the ending the *root word*. For example, in the word *hunting*, the root word is *hunt* and the ending is *-ing*.

T: What is the root word in each of these words:
cutting?   *getting?*   *sitting?*

When to double. On the board, write *cut, get, sit* in one column and *cutting, getting, sitting* in another.

T: (Point to column 2.) What letter is doubled in each of these words? [S: *t*.] What kind of letter is *t*—a vowel or a consonant? [S: A consonant.] Notice that each of these words has the same kind of letter before the *t*. What kind of letter is it? [S: A vowel.]

T: When a root word ends in a consonant with a short vowel in front of it, you must usually double the final consonant before adding *-ing*.

Write *hit* and *run* in column 1. Have S. tell you how to write *hitting* and *running*. As he answers, write these words in column 2.

When not to double. Write *hunting*, and have S. read it.

T: Is the *t* doubled in *hunting*? [S: No.] What kind of letter is in front of *t*? [S: A consonant.]

T: Remember the rule: when a word ends in two consonants, don't double the last consonant before adding *-ing*. Here are some other words that follow this rule.

Write *bringing, singing, jumping, kicking, fishing.* Have S. read each word and tell what the root word is.

Note: This note is just for your information. Do *not* explain all this to S.

The doubling rule applies to one-syllable words and final stressed syllables in longer root words (*admitting*). If the final syllable is unstressed, the final consonant is usually not doubled (*visiting*), but for some words either spelling is correct (*traveling* or *travelling*).

An exception to the doubling rule is final *x*, which is not doubled (*fixing*).

III. Writing

CHECK HOMEWORK: Page 19

Check this page with S., and have him correct any errors. Allow some time in class if he has not finished the page.

CHECKUP: Page 22

Have S. read the page title. Tell him that this is a Checkup on the new words in Lesson 3. Have him read the directions for each part. Check his work.

WRITING LESSON: Page 23

Study. Help S. study and write the words listed below, following the same procedure as in previous lessons. Call attention to these points:

1. *son.* The letter *o* is used for the sound /u/. This is a word that S. must remember. A memory aid may help, such as thinking of the round *o* as the boy's face.

2. *duck.* The letters *ck* are used for the sound /k/. When the sound /k/ is at the end of a word after a short vowel sound, it is usually written *ck*.

3. *pick.* (This word was introduced in book 1, but S. hasn't learned to spell it.) This is another word that follows the *ck* rule. Have S. tell what vowel sound comes before the sound /k/.

4. *cutting.* Two *t*'s. When a short vowel sound comes before the final consonant, double the consonant and then add *-ing*.

Listen and write. Have S. read the directions. Cover the "Study" section, and dictate these words for him to write: (1) *gun*, (2) *mud*, (3) *cut*, (4) *up*, (5) *hunting*, (6) *sun*. For *sun*, give a sentence: *The sun is high in the sky.* Check what S. wrote, and have him correct any errors.

Listen and write (last part). Cover the top two parts, and dictate these words for S. to write: (1) *cut*, (2) *cutting*, (3) *pick*, (4) *picking*, (5) *duck*, (6) *son*. For *son*, give a sentence: *Mr. Hill is with his son.* Check what S. wrote, and have him correct any errors.

HOMEWORK: Pages 24–25

Have S. read everything on page 20 aloud. Point out the capital letter at the beginning of each sentence, the period at the end, and the *-'s* in *Hill's*. Ask him to copy each sentence. Make any suggestions that S. needs to improve his writing, such as leaving space between words, keeping letters even, and making the letters stand on the bottom guidelines.

On page 25, have S. read the directions. Remind him to reread the chart and story in Lesson 4 at home.

CHECKING PROGRESS

The Homework in Lesson 3 and the Checkup in this lesson should help you evaluate your student's progress. His writing should be legible, and the words should be copied correctly. Make notes on anything he needs to practice, such as formation of letters, spacing, uniformity of size. If he had any errors in the Checkup, note the type of error, such as wrong letter or word, incorrect spelling of word, or misunderstanding directions.

MEETING INDIVIDUAL NEEDS

Reading and writing skills should be closely coordinated, as one reinforces the other. If S. is having trouble with the writing assignments, you can plan an extended period in which he can practice writing under your guidance. Or, you may want to plan two sessions for one lesson, and have him do some of the Homework in class.

If needed, use flash cards for the chart and story words in Lessons 1–3 for review. (See suggestions in those lessons.)

In *More Stories 2*, the stories for Lesson 3 may be read in class or suggested for reading at home.

Practices 4A–4D in *Focus on Phonics-2* may be used after Lesson 4. Or, you may prefer to save all of the short *u* practices to use as a review after Lesson 5.

Fill in the letters.

 city

 p i cture

 w i ndy

 Ki t ty

 l ily

 buildi n g

Fill in the words.

1. Kitty lives in the __city__.

2. It is __windy__ in the city.

3. __Jimmy__ is visiting Kitty.

4. Jimmy thanks Kitty for the __picture__.

Study.

1. son   3. pick

2. duck   4. cutting

Listen and write.

1. gun   4. up

2. mud   5. hunting

3. cut   6. sun

Listen and write.

1. cut   4. picking

2. cutting   5. duck

3. pick   6. son

Write.

This is Mr. Hill's gun.

Mr. Hill is hunting ducks.

Ed hits a duck.

The duck is in the mud.

Fill in the letters.

 g u n

 s u n

 du c k

 ri n g

 l i l y

 cut t ing

Fill in the words.

1. Ed is Mr. Hill's __son__.

2. Ed hit a __duck__.

3. The duck is in the __mud__.

4. Ed __brings__ the duck to the tent.

OBJECTIVES

To help your student:

• identify the vowel *u* and its short vowel sound /u/.

• recognize some common words in which the spelling for the sound /u/ is irregular, as in *comes, mother*.

• review the consonant blends *br* and *pr*.

• recognize the consonant blends *tr* as in *truck*, *st* as in *stuck*, *fr* as in *from*, *nk* as in *think*.

• recognize the voiced sound for *th* as in *mother, brother*.

• recognize the use of the letter *c* for the sound /k/ before the letter *o*, as in *comes*.

• review the use of *ck* for /k/ after a short vowel.

• read the following new words:
  Chart words: *truck, stuck, funny, comes, mother, brother*
  Story words: *Bud, Buck, bricks, think, from, some, does.*

• read a story, using the new chart and story words.

• summarize a story by listing the main events in the order in which they happened.

• distinguish the endings *-s, -'s, -s'*.

• write the new chart and story words.

• write sentences from dictation, using capitals and periods correctly.

INTRODUCTION

T: In this lesson, you will read some more words with the sound /u/ as in *up*.

I. Reading

CHART: Page 26

Title and key word. Have S. read the title *Lesson 5*.

T: What vowel is this lesson about? [S: *u*.]
(Point to *up*.) Read the key word. [S: up.]
(Point to *u*.) What sound does *up* begin with? [S: /u/.]

Line 1

T: Look at the first word and picture. We say this word the way it is written. What is it? [S: truck.] Good. What two consonants are at the beginning of *truck*? [S: *tr*.] Listen to the word *truck*. You hear each of the two beginning sounds, but they are blended together. This is another consonant blend.

T: (Point to t and r in column 3.) Say these two consonant sounds quickly, blending them together. [S: /tr/.] Now read the whole word. [S: truck.]

T: (Point to *ck* in column 3.) What sound do the letters *ck* stand for? [S: /k/.] Remember, if we hear the sound /k/ after a short vowel sound, it is usually written with *ck*. How many sounds are in the word? [S: Four.] How many letters? [S: Five.]

Line 2. Teach this line as you did Line 1. Call attention to the consonant blend *st* in *stuck*. Teach the consonant blend as two sounds blended together.

Line 3. Teach this line in the usual manner. Call attention to the double *n* and the vowel sound of *y* at the end of *funny*.

Line 4

T: Look at the next word and picture. Look at column 3 for help in saying the word. What is it? [S: comes.] What vowel sound do you hear in *comes*? [S: /u/.] In *comes,* the sound /u/ is written with an *o*. What sound do you hear at the end of *comes*? [S: /z/.] Good. But it is written with an *s*. What letter is silent? [S: *e*.] There are several things to remember about this word.

Have S. read the word again in column 4.

Line 5

Note: From now on, underlining will be used to distinguish the voiced sound /th/ as in *this* and *mother* from the unvoiced sound /th/ as in *think* and *thank*.

T: Look at the next picture and word. Column 3 will help you read the word. What is it? [S: mother.] What vowel sound do you hear in *mother*? [S: /u/.] How is it written? [S: With an *o*.]

T: What two consonants are in the middle? [S: *th*.] What sound did you hear for *th* in *thanks*? [S: /th/.] The sound for *th* in *mother* is almost the same. But we say it with more voice. Listen: /th/. Say /th/. [S: /th/.]

T: What sound do the letters *er* stand for? [S: /er/.]

T: How many sounds do you hear in *mother*? [S: Four.] Look back at column 2. How many letters are used to write *mother*? [S: Six.]

Have S. read the word again in column 4.

Line 6. Teach *brother* in the same way you taught *mother.* Point out the fact that *brother* and *mother* sound almost the same except for the beginning sounds. Call attention to the consonant blend *br*, the letter *o* for the sound /u/, the sound /th/ for *th*, and the sound /er/ for *er*. Ask S. how many sounds he hears in the word and how many letters it has. Have him read the word again in column 4.

Review. Have S. read all of the words again, going down the last column of the chart.

STORY: Page 27 (Uncle Bud's Truck Gets Stuck)

Have S. read the story title, and help him read the new story words.

In the first column (*Bud, Buck*), call attention to the capital letters and point out that these are names.

In the second column (*from, some, does*), have S. look at the respelling in parentheses to see how each word sounds. Call attention to the consonant blend *fr* in *from*.

In the last column, help S. read *think* as below:

T: The sound for th in this word is like the sound for *th* in *thank*. And the word ends like *thank*. Only the vowel is different. Read the word. [S: think.] The word *think* has a blend at the end: *nk*. The sound /ng/ is blended with the sound /k/. Say /ngk/. [S: /ngk/.] Now say *think*. [S: think.]

Have S. read the last word, *bricks*. Point out that it begins with the same blend, *br*, as *bring* and *brother*.

Directed silent reading. Have S. read the story silently, paragraph by paragraph, to answer these questions:

Par. 1. Who is Bud Buck?

Par. 2. How does Uncle Bud come from the city?
Why does he come?

Par. 3. What does Uncle Bud bring in his truck?
Who are the bricks for?

Par. 4. What happens to Mr. Buck's truck?
Who thinks it is funny?

Par. 5. What does Mrs. Hill tell Ed to do?
Why would they put bricks in the mud?

Par. 6. Does the truck get out of the mud?
Where does Uncle Bud bring the truck?
Who thanks Uncle Bud?

Recognizing order of events. Have S. read the whole story again silently. Then have him summarize the story by telling the main events in the order in which they happened. You may list the events as he tells them. The list might be as follows:

1. Uncle Bud comes from the city, bringing some bricks in his truck.
2. His truck gets stuck in the mud.
3. Ed thinks it is funny.
4. Mrs. Hill tells Ed to put some bricks in the mud.
5. Ed and Mrs. Hill put some bricks in the mud.
6. Uncle Bud brings the truck to the building.
7. Mrs. Hill thanks her brother for the bricks.

Word study. Have S. find these words in the story:
1. Each of the new story words.
2. The words that start with the consonant blend *br* (*brother, brings, bricks*).
3. The words that end with -*'s* (*Ed's, Hill's, Buck's*).

Punctuation review. In paragraph 5, have S. find the quotation marks and read just the part that Mrs. Hill says.

Oral reading. Have S. read the whole story aloud.

Reading between the lines. Discuss these questions.

1. What is Ed's reaction when the truck gets stuck? [He thinks it is funny.] What is Mrs. Hill's reaction? [She doesn't think it is funny.]

2. Who figures out how to get the truck out of the mud? [Mrs. Hill does.]

3. From what you have read about Ed Hill in this story and the last story about duck hunting, about how old do you think he is—10, 15, or 25? What makes you think so? [He's probably 15. He's old enough to carry a gun, but young enough to be a little silly at times. His mother doesn't talk to him as if he were an adult.]

4. Have you ever gotten stuck in mud, snow, or sand? Or, have you ever helped someone who was stuck? What did you do to get out?

II. Skills Practice

T: Please close your book. We will have some exercises on listening for vowel sounds and consonant blends. Also, we will practice some endings.

PRACTICE 1: Vowel Sounds /u/ and /i/

T: I will say three words.
Which word has the vowel sound /u/ as in *up*:
bricks, Bud, stick?   *fun, visit, him?*
uncle, not, thanks?   *stuck, think, Hill?*
city, Ed, mud?   *Jimmy, Kitty, funny?*

Write *in* and *up* on the board, and have S. read them.

T: Which of these words—*in* or *up* has the same vowel sound as the words I say:
cup, pup, lunch? [S: up.]   *bricks, him, it?*   [S: in.]
his, big, ring? [S: in.]   *mother, sun, duck?* [S: up.]
pin, tin, sick? [S: in.]   *brother, gun, does?* [S: up.]

PRACTICE 2: Beginning Consonant Blends *tr, st*

Write *truck* and *stuck*. Ask S. what consonant blend each begins with. As he answers, underline *tr* and *st*.

T: Which word begins with the consonant blend *tr*:
track, tack?   *trap, rap?*   *truck, tuck?*
tail, trail?   *rust, trust?*   *rain, train?*

T: Which word begins with the consonant blend *st*:
stuck, tuck?   *sick, stick?*   *tore, store?*
top, stop?   *stand, sand?*   *sing, sting?*

PRACTICE 3: Beginning Consonant Blends *br, pr*

Write *bring* and *pretty*. Ask S. what consonant blend each begins with. As he answers, underline *br* and *pr*.

T: I will say two words that begin with the same blend. Which blend do they begin with, *br* or *pr*:
bread, brick?   *prize, prove?*   *price, present?*
press, print?   *brush, bread?*   *bridge, brother?*

PRACTICE 4: Ending Consonant Blend *nk*

Write *think* on the board, and have S. read it.

T: *Think* ends with the consonant blend *nk*. (Draw a line under *nk*.) Read the word again. [S: think.]

T: I will say two words. Listen carefully.
Which word ends with the *nk* blend as in *think*:
thank, thick?   *bank, bang?*   *tent, tank?*
Fran, Frank?   *thing, blank?*   *wink, wing?*

PRACTICE 5: Spellings with *-k* and *-ck*

T: (Write *k* and *ck* on the board.) The sound for both of these is the same. What is it? [S: /k/.] At the end of a word, the sound /k/ is sometimes written with *k* and sometimes with *ck*. You can tell which it is by listening to the sound that comes just before the /k/ sound. If you hear a short vowel sound just before /k/, then it will be *ck*. If you hear a consonant sound just before /k/, then it will be k.

T: I will say a word. Listen carefully.
Does the word end with *k* or *ck*:
duck?   *brick?*   *milk?*   *truck?*
desk?   *back?*   *mark?*   *pick?*

PRACTICE 6: Noun Endings *-s, -'s, -s'*

Make three columns on the board with the headings *-s, -'s, -s'*. Read each of the sentences below. Have S. listen for the word with one of these endings, tell you what the word is, and what the ending is. If he gives the right answer, write the word in the correct column. If he doesn't, write the sentence for him and help him understand the meaning of the ending.

1. This is *Kim's* ring.
2. The *girls* are in the gift shop.
3. Bud is Mrs. *Hill's* brother.
4. The fish is for the *Hills'* dinner.
5. The *Hills* are fishing in the river.
6. This is the *Olivers'* kitchen.
7. Ed put some *bricks* in the mud.
8. Mr. Buck is *Ed's* uncle.

III. Writing

CHECK HOMEWORK: Pages 24–25

Check these pages with S., and have him correct any errors. Allow time in class if he hasn't finished.

WRITING LESSON: Page 28

Study. Help S. study and write these words: (1) *mother*, (2) *brother*, (3) *comes*, (4) *does*, (5) *some*, (6) *from*.

Point out that in each word the vowel sound /u/ is written with *o*. Call attention to the use of *c* for /k/ before *o* in *comes*. Point out the silent *e* in *comes* and *some*.

Study.

1. mother   4. does

2. brother   5. some

3. comes   6. from

Listen and write.

1. truck   4. brick

2. stuck   5. think

3. Buck   6. funny

Listen and write.

1. The truck is in the mud.

2. Bud is Mrs. Hill's brother.

Write.

uncle

mother

brother

truck

Ed thinks it is funny.

Mrs. Hill is Ed's mother.

Listen and write. Dictate these words for S. to write: (1) *truck,* (2) *stuck,* (3) *Buck,* (4) *brick,* (5) *think,* (6) *funny.* Check what S. has written and have him correct any errors.

Then, ask S. to cover the top two parts of the page. Dictate these sentences for him to write:

1. The truck is in the mud.
2. Bud is Mrs. Hill's brother.

Check your student's work carefully for capital letters, periods, and the use of *-'s.* Have him correct any errors.

HOMEWORK: Page 29

Ask S. to read the title, words, and sentences. Have him say the names of the letters in *uncle.* Call attention to the *c* for /k/ and the *le* for /ul/. Explain that *uncle* is written with a capital *U* when it is used with a name, such as *Uncle Bud,* but otherwise it is written with a small *u,* as in *an uncle, his uncle, my uncle.*

Ask S. to write the words and sentences at home. Give any suggestions that will improve his writing. Encourage him to reread Lessons 4–5 about the short sound for *u.*

CHECKING PROGRESS

For a quick review to check progress, have S. read aloud a certain paragraph from each of the first four stories. Then ask him a question, or have him tell the main idea in his own words. Note the following:

1. Does he recognize what a paragraph is?
2. Can he locate the designated paragraph?
3. Does he understand the main idea?
4. Does he recognize most of the words?
5. Does he observe punctuation marks?
6. Does he read fluently?

MEETING INDIVIDUAL NEEDS

Use flash cards for the new chart and story words in Lessons 4–5. See the suggestions in Lesson 1 for the way to make the cards and use them.

Make a separate flash card for each word needed to make the following sentences:

Ed is the Hills' son.   Mr. Buck is Ed's uncle.
She is Ed's mother.   He is Mrs. Hill's brother.

Mix up the word cards for one sentence. Dictate the sentence, and have S. arrange the words in the right order. Do this for each sentence.

In *More Stories 2,* the stories for Lesson 4 may be read in class or suggested for reading at home.

Practices 5A–5E in *Focus on Phonics 2* may be used after Lesson 5. Or, if you have saved all of the short *u* practices to use as a review, you may do them now. Another possibility is to save all of *Focus on Phonics 2* to use after completing book 2.

LESSON 6

Book 2
Pages 30–35

OBJECTIVES

To help your student:

- recognize the vowel *e* and its associated short sound /e/ as in *egg*.
- recognize the consonant blends *tw* as in *twelve* and *fr* as in *fresh*.
- review the use of the ending -*s* as a noun plural (as in *eggs*) and as a verb ending (as in *sells*).
- read the following new words:
  Chart words: *bell, hens, cents, help, twelve, seventy*
  Story words: *Fred, fresh, very, Ellen, will, many*.
- read a story, using the new chart and story words.
- interpret the main idea of the story by summarizing.
- recognize direct quotations.
- review the use of the question mark.
- read orally with expression.
- write the new chart and story words.
- write a question, using the question mark.

INTRODUCTION

T: Today we will have a lesson about another vowel.

I. Reading

CHART: Page 30

Title and key word. Have S. read the title *Lesson 6*.

T: What vowel is this lesson about? [S: *e*.]
(Point to *egg*.) Read the key word. [S: egg.]
(Point to *e*.) What sound does egg begin with? [S: /e/.]

Lines 1–6

T: This lesson has many new words with the vowel sound /e/. Most of the words in the chart are pronounced the way they are written. Study the chart, and read the words to yourself. Look at column 3 if you need help.

After S. has studied the chart silently, have him read each word aloud. Call attention to these points:

1. Which word ends with a double consonant? [S: bell.]
2. Which word has a silent e on the end? [S: twelve.]
3. What is the sound for c in *cents*? [S: /s/.]
4. Which word ends with a vowel sound for *y*? [S: seventy.]
5. Which word has two consonants at the beginning? [S: twelve.] Listen to the word *twelve*. Do you hear the sound for both *t* and *w*? [S: Yes.] The two sounds blend together. This is another consonant blend. We call it the *tw* blend. (Point to *tw*.) What is the blend? [S: *tw*.] Read the word again. [S: twelve.]

Review. Have S. read all of the words again, going down the last column of the chart.

STORY: Page 31 (Eggs to Sell)

Have S. read the story title, and help him read the new story words. In the first column, point out the consonant blend *fr* in *Fred* and *fresh*. Have S. read the other new words (*Ellen, will, very, many*) to himself and then aloud. Help him sound out the words if necessary. Ask him which of the new words are names.

Directed silent reading. Have S. read the story silently, paragraph by paragraph, to answer these questions:

Par. 1. What does Ellen Bell sell?
Par. 2. How does Ellen's son help her?
Par. 3. What kind of eggs does Ms. Bell sell?
How much does she sell twelve eggs for?
Par. 4. What is Fred King's question?
Par. 5. What is Ellen Bell's answer?
Par. 6. What does Fred give to Ellen?
Par. 7. What is Fred's next question?
Par. 8. Who will get a hen for Fred?

Summarizing. Have S. read the whole story again silently. Then ask him to summarize the story in his own words. Stress that, in summarizing, he should tell just the main ideas. His summary might be as follows:

[Ellen Bell sells eggs and hens. Her son helps her. Fred King looks at the eggs. He asks if they are fresh. Ellen says they are. Fred gets twelve eggs for seventy cents. Ellen's son will get a hen for Fred.]

Oral reading. Ask S. to find the part in paragraph 4 that Fred King says. Have him point out the quotation marks and question mark. Then have him read the question aloud.

Have S. find the other question that Fred asked. Ask him how he knows that it is a question. Have him read it aloud.

It may be helpful for S. if you read the part of one of the characters and have him read the other part. Then reverse parts. Encourage S. to read with expression.

Finally, have S. read the whole story aloud.

Reading between the lines. Discuss the questions that relate directly to the story plus any other questions that you think would be of interest to S.

1. Did Fred King buy a dozen eggs? [Yes.] How do you know? [The story said he got *twelve* eggs.] (If S. doesn't know that *dozen* means twelve, explain this.)
2. If Fred gave Ellen a dollar for a dozen eggs, how much change would he get? [Thirty cents.] If he bought two dozen eggs, how much would he pay? [$1.40.] (You may skip these questions if they would be too hard for S.)
3. Compare the price of eggs in the story with prices at stores in your area (and at roadside stands or farmers' markets, if there are any). If possible, bring some store ads. Talk about different sizes of eggs and their prices.

---

4. Discuss the nutritional value of eggs and how eggs, cheese, and beans can be used as substitutes for meat.

5. If a person works for a family member, as Ellen's son does, should he or she be paid the same as any other employee? Why or why not?

II. Skills Practice

T: Please close your book. We will have some practice exercises on listening for the vowel sound /e/ and some consonant blends. We will also have an exercise on adding the -s ending to some words.

PRACTICE 1: Vowel Sound /e/

T: Listen to these words.
Which one has the vowel sound /e/ as in *egg:*
Ed, Bud? *Ellen, Jill?* *Fran, Fred?*
bill, bell? *fish, fresh?* *bet, bit?*

PRACTICE 2: Beginning Consonant Blends *tw, fr*

T: (Write *twelve,* and have S. read it.) What consonant sounds do you hear before the vowel sound in *twelve*? [S: /tw/.] Good. The two sounds are blended together. (Underline *tw.*) What do you call this blend? [S: *tw.*]

T: Which word begins with the consonant blend *tw:*
ten, twenty? *twin, win?* *test, twice?*
twelve, tell? *west, twist?* *witch, twitch?*

T: (Write *fresh,* and have S. read it.) What consonant sounds do you hear before the vowel sound in *fresh*? [S: /fr/.] Good. The two sounds are blended together. (Underline *fr.*) What do we call this blend? [S: *fr.*]

T: Which word begins with the consonant blend *fr*:
from, fun? *Fran, ran?* *free, tree?*
fresh, fish? *red, Fred?* *find, friend?*

PRACTICE 3: Ending -s

Noun plural -s. Write *eggs, hens, cents* in a column. Have S. read them. Ask him what ending is on these words. Then have him tell what each word would be without the -s ending. Write each word without -s as he says it.

Ask S. what the -s ending means [more than one]. Then have him give a sentence using each word as you point to *hens, egg, cents, eggs, cent, hen.*

Verb ending -s. Write *sells, gets, helps* in a column. Have S. read them. Then ask him what each word would be without the -s ending. Write the word without -s as he says it.

36   Lesson 6

T: In these words, the -s ending doesn't mean more than one. The words *sell, get,* and *help* are action words. An action word tells what someone does.

T: We use the -s ending on an action word after *he, she, it* or after any word that can take the place of *he, she,* or *it* in the sentence. Listen to these examples.

T: He sells eggs. Bob sells eggs. The man sells eggs.
She helps me. Ann helps me. The woman helps me.
It gets stuck. The truck gets stuck.

Follow this procedure to continue the exercise:

1. Write this sentence with a blank for the action word. Under the blank, write both forms of the word.
   Fred _____ some eggs.
   　　　　get, gets

2. Read the complete sentence, *Fred gets some eggs,* aloud to S. Have him tell whether he heard *get* or *gets*. If necessary, repeat the sentence.

3. Have S. write the correct form of the word in the sentence and then read the sentence aloud.

Continue in a similar way with the sentences listed below. Some students may be able to choose the correct form of the verb without your reading the sentence first. But, if S. does not commonly pronounce the -s ending on verbs, it is very important to let him *hear* the correct form in the sentence before he is asked to identify the correct form and write it.

Ellen _____ a box.	*(get, gets)*
The girls _____ Ed.	*(help, helps)*
The Hills _____ some fish.	*(get, gets)*
Ms. Bell _____ hens.	*(sell, sells)*
Her son _____ her.	*(help, helps)*
I _____ trucks.	*(sell, sells)*

III. Writing

CHECK HOMEWORK: Page 29

Check this page with S. Be sure to note whether he has used capitals, periods, and -'s in the right places. Have him correct any errors.

CHECKUP: Page 32

Have S. read the directions. Have him do the first part of the page and check it. Then have him do the second part and check it. Help him correct any errors.

WRITING LESSON: Page 33

Study. Help S. study and write these words: (1) *twelve,* (2) *cents,* (3) *seventy,* (4) *very.* Call attention to the *tw* blend and silent *e* in *twelve,* the *c* for /s/ in *cents,* and the *y* at the end of *seventy* and *very.*

Listen and write. Dictate these words for S. to write: (1) *egg,* (2) *bell,* (3) *hens,* (4) *help,* (5) *yes,* (6) *fresh.* Check his work, and have him correct any errors.

Then have S. cover the top two parts of the page, and dictate these sentences for him to write.

1. Ellen Bell sells eggs.
2. Her son helps her.
3. Fred gets twelve eggs.
4. Ellen gets seventy cents.

Check your student's work, giving careful attention to capitals, periods, and the -s ending. Correct any mistakes in a positive way.

WRITING LESSON: Page 34

Tell S. that he will change each sentence to a question and write the question. The first one is done for him. Have him read the first sentence aloud and tell what punctuation mark is at the end [period]. Then have him read the question and tell what punctuation mark is at the end [question mark].

Demonstrate how to write the question mark. Have S. practice on unlined paper and then trace the question mark in his book.

Have S. read sentence 2 aloud, change it to a question orally, and then write the question. Check his work, and have him correct any errors.

Finish the page in the same way. If S. has difficulty changing a sentence to a question, dictate the question to him and have him write it.

HOMEWORK: Page 35

Have S. read the title and directions aloud. Ask him to do this at home and to reread the chart and story.

CHECKING PROGRESS

The Checkup in this lesson will tell you if S. can distinguish the vowel sounds /u/ and /i/ and can write the correct letters for /th/, /k/, and /er/. If he made any errors, say the word and have him listen for that sound and tell what letter or letters stand for it. Note whether his difficulty is in hearing the sound or in writing the letters. Use other words for the same sound.

Use flash cards for the chart and story words in Lessons 1–5 to see if S. knows them by sight. He should be learning to recognize by sight the words that he first read by blending the sounds. He should not have to sound out a word each time he sees it.

MEETING INDIVIDUAL NEEDS

If there are any words from Lessons 1–5 that S. doesn't recognize fairly quickly, help him to blend the sounds and read the words. Note which sound-symbol relationships need work. Give extra practice with flash cards. You may also let S. take the cards home to study.

In *More Stories 2,* the stories for Lesson 5 may be read in class or suggested for reading at home.

Practices 6A–6C in *Focus on Phonics 2* may be used after Lesson 6. Or, you may prefer to save all of the short *e* practices to use as a review after Lesson 7.

Checkup

Fill in the letters.

 tr**u**ck    f**u**nny

 br**i**cks   mo**t**her

 stu**ck**   hunt**i n g**

Fill in the words.

1. Bud is Mrs. Hill's **brother**.

2. Bud **comes** from the city.

3. The truck gets stuck in the **mud**.

4. Ed **thinks** it is funny.

Writing Lesson

Study.

1. twelve   3. seventy

2. cents   4. very

Listen and write.

1. egg   4. help

2. bell   5. yes

3. hens   6. fresh

Listen and write.

1. Ellen Bell sells eggs.

2. Her son helps her.

3. Fred gets twelve eggs.

4. Ellen gets seventy cents.

Lesson 6   33

Writing Lesson

1. The eggs are fresh.

Are the eggs fresh?

2. The eggs are in a box.

Are the eggs in a box?

3. Ellen will sell eggs.

Will Ellen sell eggs?

4. Fred will get a hen.

Will Fred get a hen?

5. Fred is getting some eggs.

Is Fred getting some eggs?

34   Lesson 6

Homework

Fill in the letters.

 h**e**ns   c**e**nts

 e**g g**   tw**e**lve

 be**l l**   **70** s**e**venty

Fill in the words.

1. This is Ellen **Bell**.

2. She sells **hens** and **eggs**.

3. Her son **helps** her.

4. Fred gives seventy **cents** to **Ellen**.

Lesson 6   35

© New Readers Press. All rights reserved.

LESSON 7

Book 2
Pages 36–39

OBJECTIVES

To help your student:

- identify the vowel *e* and its short sound /e/.
- recognize words that rhyme, such as *bed* and *red*.
- review the consonant blends *br, fr, pr, tr*.
- review the voiced sound of *th* as in *them*.
- recognize the ending consonant blends *nt* and *nd*.
- review the verb endings *-s* and *-ing*.
- read the following new words:
  Chart words: *men, bed, red, send, friends, letter*
  Story words: *them, well, sits, quickly, side, women.*
- read a story, using the new chart and story words.
- recognize a paragraph and state its main idea.
- write the new chart and story words.
- learn correct placement of address and return address on an envelope.

INTRODUCTION

T: In today's lesson, you will have some more words with the vowel sound /e/ as in *egg*.

I. Reading

CHART: Page 36

Title and key word. Have S. read the lesson title, name of vowel, and key word. Have him give the short sound for the vowel.

Lines 1–6

T: This lesson has many new words with the vowel sound /e/. Most of the words are pronounced just the way they are written. Only one word in the chart is changed to help you read it. Study the chart, and read the words to yourself.

After S. has studied the chart silently, have him read each word aloud. Call attention to these points:

1. The similarity between *bed* and *red*. Tell S. that we call these rhyming words. Give these other examples: *sell* and *tell, men* and *hen*.
2. The *fr* blend and the silent *i* in *friends*.
3. The double *t* and the letters *er* for /er/ in *letter*.

Review. Have S. read all of the words again, going down the last column of the chart.

STORY: Page 37 (Get Well Quickly!)

Have S. read the story title and the new words. Help him sound out any words with which he needs help.

Directed silent reading. Ask S. how many paragraphs there are in the story [eight]. Then remind him that a paragraph is a group of sentences about one main idea.

Have S. read each paragraph silently and then tell what it is about. His answer should give the main idea as listed below for each paragraph, but it may not be in these exact words.

Par. 1. Fred's friends visit him when he is sick.
Par. 2. Fred sits up in bed to visit with them.
Par. 3. The men give Fred some apples.
Par. 4. The women give him some fresh eggs.
Par. 5. Fred thanks his friends.
Par. 6. His friends tell him to get well quickly.
Par. 7. Fred is not very sick.
Par. 8. Fred will send letters to his friends.

Word study. Have S. find these words in the story:

1. Each of the new story words.
2. Two words that rhyme with *bed* (*Fred, red*).
3. Two words that begin with the *fr* blend (*friends, fresh*).

Punctuation review. Have S. find each of these punctuation marks in the story: period, comma, quotation marks, exclamation point, question mark.

Oral reading. Have S. read aloud the part that the friends say in paragraph 6. Remind him to observe the quotation marks and read just the part between them. Ask him to read the two questions in paragraph 7. Then have him read the whole story aloud.

Reading between the lines. Discuss these questions:

1. How many friends in all visited Fred? [Four.]
2. How did Fred's friends show that they appreciated him? [They visited him and brought gifts.] How did Fred show his appreciation? [He thanked them when they were there, and he will send letters to them.]
3. When you are sick, do you like people to visit you? What are some things to remember when you visit someone who is sick?

Addressing an envelope. Show S. an envelope that you have prepared before class with the correct placement of address and return address. Use your own name and address as the return address. Address the letter to:

> Miss Ann Hunt
> 425 Hill Street
> Garden City, NY 11530

Explain to S. that *NY* stands for New York. Have him read the address. Point to the return address, and tell him that it is your address. If you think he can read it, let him do so. Otherwise, read it to him.

Give S. a blank envelope or a piece of paper the size of an envelope. (It may be easier for S. to write on a large business-size envelope than on a smaller one.) Ask him to copy the address for Miss Ann Hunt. Then have him write his own name and address for the return address.

Next, have S. address another envelope. Use the name Mr. Fred King and a local address with the appropriate zip code. Write this address for S. to copy. He should use his own name and address for the return address.

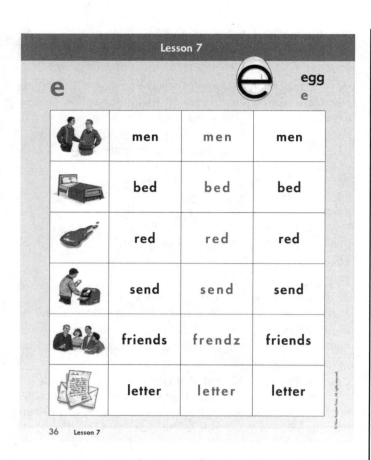

II. Skills Practice

T: Today we will have some practice exercises on listening to the three vowel sounds that we have had so far in this book. Also, we will review some of the consonant blends and endings.

PRACTICE 1: Vowel Sounds /i/, /u/, /e/

Write *i, u, e* on the board. Have S. give the short vowel sound and the key word for each. Write *in, up, egg* as he says each word.

T: Which of these keys words—*in, up, egg*—has the same vowel sound as the words I say:

pin, fish, big?	[S: in.]	*Ed, tent, bell?*	[S: egg.]
cup, bug, mud?	[S: up.]	*six, fit, this?*	[S: in.]
leg, red, them?	[S: egg.]	*duck, hunt, run?*	[S: up.]

On the board, write the words with blanks as shown in the first column. Say each sentence shown in the second column, emphasizing the word in italics. Repeat the word. Then have S. tell you what the missing vowel is. Write the letter in the blank when S. says it.

T. writes:	T. says:	T. repeats:	S. says:
p—t	I will *pet* my dog.	*pet*	[S: *e.*]
p—n	I will *pin* it together.	*pin*	[S: *i.*]
b—g	I got a *bug* in my ear.	*bug*	[S: *u.*]
l—t	I *lit* a match.	*lit*	[S: *i.*]
B—ll	I know Mr. *Bell.*	*Bell*	[S: *e.*]
st—ck	The car got *stuck.*	*stuck*	[S: *u.*]

When you have filled in all the blanks, have S. read all of the words. (Save the column of words for the next exercise.)

Explain to S. that we can make a new word by changing the vowel in each of these words. Then, follow these steps: Read the original word. Point to the vowel and tell how to change it, as shown below. Write the new word next to the old one. Have S. read the new word.

T. reads:	T. says:	T. writes:	S. reads:
pet	Change the *e* to *i.*	*pit*	[S: pit.]
pin	Change the *i* to e.	*pen*	[S: pen.]
bug	Change the *u* to *i.*	*big*	[S: big.]
lit	Change the *i* to e.	*let*	[S: let.]
Bell	Change the *e* to *i.*	*Bill*	[S: Bill.]
stuck	Change the *u* to *i.*	*stick*	[S: stick.]

PRACTICE 2: Beginning Blends *br, fr, pr, tr*

Write *bring, friend, pretty, truck*. Have S. read the words and tell what consonant blend each begins with. As he answers, underline the blends *br, fr, pr, tr*.

T: (Write *br, fr.*)
I will say two words that begin with the same blend. Which blend do they begin with, *br* or *fr*:

fresh, from?	*bridge, brown?*	*friend, fry?*
bring, brick?	*front, freeze?*	*brush, bread?*

T: (Write *pr, tr.*) This time, I will say two words that begin with one of these blends.
Which blend do they begin with, *pr* or *tr*:

pretty, prize?	*trash, trick?*	*print, prize?*
truck, trip?	*press, price?*	*trap, trust?*

PRACTICE 3: Consonant Sound /th/ as in *them*

Write *them* on the board, and have S. read it.

T: What two letters are at the beginning of *them*? [S: *th*.] These two letters stand for one sound. The sound for *th* in *them* is the same as it is in *mother*. What is the sound? [S: /th/.] Good. This is the *th* sound that we make with more voice.

T: Which word starts with the sound /th/ as in *them*:

Tim, they?	*stick, this?*	*Dan, then?*
that, what?	*then, ten?*	*that, zip?*

PRACTICE 4: Ending Blends *nt, nd*

T: (Write *hunt* on the board.) Read the word. [S: hunt.] *Hunt* ends with the consonant blend *nt*. (Underline *nt*.)

T: Which word ends with the *nt* blend:

hot, hunt?	*pant, pat?*	*went, when?*
cent, sit?	*ten, tent?*	*plant, plan?*

T: (Write *send* on the board.) Read the word. [S: send.] *Send* ends with the consonant blend *nd*. (Underline *nd*.)

T: Which word ends with the *nd* blend:

had, hand?	*win, wind?*	*friend, Fran?*
bend, bed?	*cent, send?*	*Fred, friend?*

PRACTICE 5: Verb ending *-ing*

Review of doubling and not doubling. Write these words in a column: *tell, send, help, think, get, sit, run*. Have S. read each word. Review the rules for adding *-ing*:
1. When a root word ends in two consonants, don't double the last consonant before adding *-ing*.
2. When a root word ends in a consonant with a short vowel in front of it, you must usually double the last consonant before adding *-ing*.

Have S. tell you how to write each word with *-ing*. As he answers, write the *-ing* form next to the root word.

Write *visit, visiting*. Have S. read both words. Tell him that this is a word that doesn't follow these rules.

Dropping final silent *e* before *-ing*. Write *come, give* in one column and *coming, giving* in another. Explain that we drop the final silent *e* before adding *-ing*.

Write *live, have* in column 1. Have S. tell you how to write *living* and *having*. As he answers, write these words in column 2.

PRACTICE 6: Verb Ending *-s*

Using all of the root words in Practice 5, have S. tell you what each word would be with *-s* and how to write it. As he answers, write the word.

III. Writing

CHECK HOMEWORK: Page 35

Check this page with S., and have him correct any errors.

WRITING LESSON: Page 38

Study. Help S. study and write these words: (1) *letter*, (2) *friends*, (3) *women*, (4) *quickly*.

Listen and write. Dictate these words for S. to write: (1) *men*, (2) *bed*, (3) *red*, (4) *well*, (5) *them*, (6) *sick*, (7) *sits*, (8) *visit*.

Check your student's work. Have him correct any errors. Then have him cover the top two parts of the page. Dictate these sentences for him to write:
1. Fred is sick in bed.
2. Is Fred very sick?
3. Get well quickly.

Check the sentences with S., giving careful attention to the correct use of capitals, periods, and question mark. Praise him for what he has done right. Make constructive suggestions for improvement, if needed.

HOMEWORK: Page 39

Go over the directions with S. Explain that in the second exercise he should fill in the blanks with words from the story. If there is any word he doesn't know how to spell, he may look back at the story and find it.

Suggest that S. practice addressing an envelope. He can practice on a piece of paper and bring it along next time. Encourage him to reread all the stories he has had so far in this book.

CHECKING PROGRESS

The exercises in the Skills Practice for this lesson should help you check your student's progress in these skills:
—distinguishing vowel sounds /e/, /i/, /u/.
—identifying consonant blends *br, fr, pr, tr*.
—identifying the voiced sound /th/ as in *that*.
—adding verb endings *-s* and *-ing* to known words.

If most of your student's responses in these exercises were accurate, you may consider his progress satisfactory.

Study.

1. letter   3. women

2. friends   4. quickly

Listen and write.

1. men   5. them

2. bed   6. sick

3. red   7. sits

4. well   8. visit

Write.

1. Fred is sick in bed.

2. Is Fred very sick?

3. Get well quickly.

Fill in the letters.

m e n   s e nd

le t ter   kitchen

b e d   c utting

Fill in the words.

1. His friends give him some eggs and apples.

2. Fred will get well.

3. He will send letters to the men and women.

Use flash cards for the chart and story words in Lesson 6 to check your student's sight recognition.

Note your student's writing in the Writing Lesson and Homework for the last three lessons. Is it legible? Are most letters formed correctly? Does your student use capital letters and punctuation marks correctly?

If S. needs quite a lot of extra practice on these skills, you may want to plan a supplementary lesson for the next time. If his progress on the whole is satisfactory, let him go on to Lesson 8.

MEETING INDIVIDUAL NEEDS

If S. needs more practice in distinguishing vowel sounds, these two exercises may be helpful:

1. Mix up the flash cards for the chart and story words from Lessons 1–6. Ask S. to sort the words into piles according to the vowel sound in the word: /e/, /i/, /u/, or /y/. (Ask him to put the words with /y/ in a separate pile even though they have an additional vowel sound.) He should sort the cards by the *sound* of the vowel, not by its name.

2. Make a small card for each of these vowels: *e, i, u.* Then make a second set of cards, leaving a blank for the missing vowel in these words:

b___g	b___t	b___ll	tr___ck
p___n	h___m	d___ck	st___ck

Working with one word card at a time, dictate different words that can be formed with different vowels. Have S. select the vowel card to match the word you dictate, put it in the blank, and then read the word. These are the words you can dictate:

big, bug	*but, bit*	*bell, bill*	*truck, trick*
pen, pin	*him, hum*	*duck, deck*	*stick, stuck*

In *More Stories 2*, the stories for Lesson 6 may be read in class or suggested for reading at home.

Practices 7A–7F in *Focus on Phonics 2* may be used after Lesson 7. Or, if you have saved all of the short *e* practices to use as a review, you may do them now. Another possibility is to save all of *Focus on Phonics 2* to use after completing book 2.

LESSON 8

OBJECTIVES

To help your student:
- recognize the vowel *a* and its associated short sound /a/ as in *apple*.
- recognize that words rhyme when they end with the same combination of vowel and consonant sounds, such as /at/ in *cat* and *rat*.
- recognize the consonant blends *bl* as in *black* and *sm* as in *Smith*.
- review the consonant blend *st* as in *standing*.
- recognize the use of *c* for the sound /k/ before the letter *a* as in *cat* and *can*.
- review the use of *ck* for /k/ after a short vowel.
- recognize the root word of words ending in *-ing*, such as *standing* and *carrying*.
- read the following new words in two charts and stories:
  Chart words: *cat, rat, bat, back, black, standing*
  Story words: *that, can, cannot, kill, Smith, quick*

  Chart words: *bag, basket, happy, marry, carrying, family*
  Story word: *Jack*.
- read two stories, using the new chart and story words.
- understand the main idea of a paragraph.
- understand the main idea of a story.
- recognize the emotions of characters in a story.
- write the new chart and story words.

INTRODUCTION

T: Today's lesson is about another vowel sound. Please turn to page 40, and find out what it is.

I. Reading

CHART: Page 40

Title and key word. Have S. read the lesson title, name of vowel, and key word. Have him give the short sound for the vowel: /a/.

Lines 1–6. Tell S. that all of the words in the chart are pronounced the way they are written. Have him study the chart and read the words to himself. When he has finished, have him read each word aloud. Then ask these questions:

1. What three words end with the sound /t/ as in *tent*? [S: cat, rat, bat.]
2. What is the vowel sound before /t/ in *cat, rat, bat*? [S: /a/.] When words end with the same combination of vowel and consonant sounds, we say they rhyme. In these words, the combination is /at/. Can you think of any words not on the chart that rhyme with *cat*? [Possible answers: *fat, hat, mat, pat, sat, that, flat*.]

3. Which word in the chart rhymes with *back*? [S: black.]
4. Why is the sound /k/ at the end of *back* and *black* written with *ck*? [S: /k/ comes after a short vowel sound.]
5. How many consonant sounds do you hear before /a/ in *back*? [S: One.] What is the sound? [S: /b/.]

   How many consonant sounds do you hear before /a/ in *black*? [S: Two.] What are they? [S: /bl/.] What are the letters? [S: *bl*.] We call this the *bl* blend.
6. Look at the word *standing*. What is the blend at the beginning of the word? [S: *st*.] What would the word be without the *-ing* ending? [S: stand.]
7. What letter is used for the sound /k/ in *cat*? [S: *c*.] What letter comes after the *c*? [S: *a*.]

Review. Have S. read all of the words again, going down the last column of the chart.

STORY: Page 41 (The Rat)

Have S. read the story title and the new words. Call attention to these points in the new words:
1. The voiced sound /th/ for *th* in *that*.
2. The use of *c* for /k/ before *a* in *can*.
3. The two words in *cannot*: *can* and *not*. (Do not use the term *compound word* at this point, however.)
4. The capital *S* in *Smith* to show it is a name.
5. The consonant blend *sm* in *Smith*. (This is new.)

Directed silent reading

T: Read the first paragraph to yourself, and find out the names of the people in the story. [S: reads.] What are the names? [S: Ann Smith, Sam Smith, and Dan Smith.] Who are Sam and Dan? [S: Ann's brothers.] Which one is the little brother? [S: Dan.]

Have S. read the rest of the story silently and then tell in his own words what happened in the story.

Reading between the lines. Discuss these questions.

1. How do you think Dan feels in the story? [Excited.] What shows that he is excited? [He yells.] How do you think Ann feels? [Excited.]
2. Do you think Ann was afraid or not? (Bring out the point that we can't tell for sure if she was afraid or not. But, even if she was, she took command and told her brothers what to do.)
3. Does Ann seem to be older or younger than her two brothers? [The story says that Dan is the little brother. Ann seems to be older than Sam, too, because she's the one who takes charge, and he obeys her.]

Word study. Have S. read the new story words aloud. Ask him which one rhymes with *cat* [*that*]. Have him find each of the words in the story.

Punctuation review. Ask S. to find each of the following punctuation marks: quotation marks, exclamation point, period, comma. Review what each of these means.

a

apple
a

	cat	cat	cat
	rat	rat	rat
	bat	bat	bat
	back	back	back
	black	black	black
	standing	standing	standing

The Rat

that	kill
can	Smith
cannot	quick

That woman is Ann Smith.
That is Ann's brother Sam Smith.
That is Ann's little brother Dan Smith.

Ann is standing in the kitchen.
Sam is standing in the kitchen.
Dan is standing in the kitchen.
Ann is standing with her back to the boys.

Dan hits Ann on the back.
Dan yells, "A rat! A rat!
A rat is in back of that black box."

Ann yells, "Quick, Sam, bring a bat!
I can kill the rat."

Sam brings his bat.
He gives it to Ann.
Ann says, "I will kill that rat.
Quick, Sam, pick up that black box."

Sam picks up the black box.
The rat runs quickly.
Ann cannot hit the rat.

Ann says, "I will get a cat.
A cat can kill the rat."

Sam says, "A cat cannot kill a rat."

Ann says, "That is a little rat.
A big cat can kill a little rat."

a

apple
a

	bag	bag	bag
	basket	basket	basket
	happy	happy	happy
	marry	marry	marry
	carrying	carrying	carrying
	family	family	family

Jack and Ann Will Marry

Jack

This is the Smith family.
The Smith family lives in the city.

That man is Jack Black.
Jack Black lives in the valley.
Jack is visiting the Smith family.

Sam Smith is carrying Jack's bag.
Sam is carrying the bag in his hand.
He is carrying the bag for Jack.

Jack is carrying a basket.
It is a basket of apples.
Jack is carrying the basket of apples.
He is bringing the apples to the Smith family.

Jack will marry Ann Smith.
Ann will marry Jack Black.
Jack and Ann will marry.

Jack and Ann are happy.
Mr. and Mrs. Smith are happy.
Ann's brothers are happy.
Sam is happy that Ann will marry Jack.
Dan is happy that Ann will marry Jack.
The Smith family is happy.

Oral reading. Ask S. to read the parts that Dan and Sam say while you read the part of Ann. Then reverse parts. Encourage S. to read with expression and to observe the punctuation marks.

CHART: Page 42

Explain that, in this lesson, there are two charts about the vowel *a*. Have S. read the name of the vowel and key word. Have him give the short sound for the vowel.

Lines 1–6. Tell S. that all of the words in this chart are pronounced the way they are written. Have him study the chart and read the words to himself. When he has finished, have him read each word aloud. Then ask these questions:

1. Which words end with *y*? [S: happy, marry, family.] In these words, is *y* a vowel or a consonant? [S: A vowel.]
2. Which word ends with the ending *-ing*? [S: carrying.] What would the word be without the *-ing*? [S: carry.]
3. Which words have double consonants? [S: happy, marry, carrying.]

Review. Have S. read all of the words again, going down the last column of the chart.

STORY: Page 43 (Jack and Ann Will Marry)

Have S. read the story title and the new word *Jack*. Call attention to the capital *J* at the beginning of the name and the *ck* after the short vowel sound.

Directed silent reading. Have S. read each paragraph silently and then tell you what the main idea is. His answers should be similar to these statements:

Par. 1. The Smith family lives in the city.
Par. 2. Jack Black is visiting the Smith family.
Par. 3. Sam is carrying Jack's bag.
Par. 4. Jack is bringing apples to the Smiths.
Par. 5. Jack Black and Ann Smith will marry.
Par. 6. The Smith family is happy.

T: What do you think is the main idea of the whole story? [S: Jack and Ann will marry.] Good. It is the same as the title of the story.

Oral reading. Have S. read the whole story aloud.

Reading between the lines. Discuss these questions.

1. How many people are there in the Smith family? [Five.]
2. Is Jack coming to visit the Smith family just for the day or will he stay overnight? How do you know? [He'll stay overnight because he's bringing his bag.]

Relating the stories to everyday life. You may wish to discuss these points in relation to the two stories.

1. What are some reasons for getting rid of rats? What are the best ways to get rid of them? What safety measures should be followed when rat poison is used?
2. What are some things that an engaged couple does to get ready for their wedding?

II. Skills Practice

T: Please close your book. We will have some listening exercises on consonant blends and rhyming words. Also, we will have an exercise on the ending *-ing*.

PRACTICE 1: Beginning Consonant Blends *bl, st, sm*

Write the blends *bl, st, sm* on the board, and have S. tell what they are.

T: Which word begins with the consonant blend *bl*: *blank, bank?*   *bring, blue?*   *black, brown?*

T: Which word begins with the consonant blend *st*: *stand, sand?*   *stick, sick?*   *shop, stop?*

T: Which word begins with the consonant blend *sm*: *smell, shell?*   *smoke, soak?*   *smart, start?*

PRACTICE 2: Rhyming Words
T: (Write *cat*, and have S. read it.)
Which word rhymes with *cat*:
can, hat?   *fat, fit?*   *bat, bad?*   *sack, sat?*
T: (Write *back*, and have S. read it.)
Which word rhymes with *back*:
pick, pack?   *sack, sick?*   *stuck, stack?*   *trick, track?*

PRACTICE 3: Dropping the Ending *-ing*

Say each of the following words, and have S. tell what the word would be without the *-ing* ending:

marrying	singing	kicking	getting	coming
carrying	bringing	looking	cutting	giving
jumping	standing	helping	hunting	fishing

III. Writing

CHECK HOMEWORK: Page 39

Check this page with S. Have him correct any errors. Also, check the "envelope" if he addressed one as suggested.

WRITING LESSON: Page 44

Explain that there is no "Study" section because the words in both charts are written the way they sound. Instead, there are two longer "Listen and write" sections.

Listen and write (words). Dictate these words for S. to write: (1) *cat*, (2) *Jack*, (3) *back*, (4) *black*, (5) *rat*, (6) *that*, (7) *standing*, (8) *basket*.

Help S. check his work and correct any errors.

Listen and write (sentences). Have S. cover the top half of the page. Then dictate these sentences for him to write:

1. That is a little rat.
2. Dan is standing with Sam.
3. Sam is carrying Jack's bag.
4. Ann will marry Jack Black.
5. The Smith family is happy.

Listen and Write

1. cat - - - - - - - - 5. rat - - - - - -
2. Jack - - - - - 6. that - - - - -
3. back - - - - - - 7. standing - - -
4. black - - - - - - 8. basket - - - -

Listen and Write

1. That is a little rat. - - - - - -
2. Dan is standing with Sam. - - -
3. Sam is carrying Jack's bag. - -
4. Ann will marry Jack Black. - - -
5. The Smith family is happy. - -

Fill in the letters.

bag - - -   family

basket - -   marry

carry - - -   happy

Fill in the words.

That - - cat - is black. - - -

The - - rat - - is little. - - - -

This is Sam's - back - . - - -

Check the sentences with S., giving careful attention to capitals, periods, and 's in *Jack's*. Have him correct any errors. Give positive suggestions that may help him improve his writing or spelling.

HOMEWORK: Page 45

Go over the directions with S. Also, ask him to read both charts and stories over again at home.

CHECKING PROGRESS

Check your student's progress in oral reading by having him read a paragraph from each story in Lessons 5–7. Note his ability to read fluently and with expression. Does he observe the punctuation marks? Does he omit any words or make substitutions? Does he hesitate on any words or repeat words? Do you have to tell him a word?

If S. makes any errors, note what type they are, but don't mention them while he is reading. You can give extra practice to help with particular needs later on.

To check your student's progress in comprehension skills, you may have him read new material using old words. A story from *More Stories 2* would serve this purpose. After

he has read the story silently, ask several factual questions about it. S. should be able to answer most of your questions about important points in the story. If he doesn't remember an answer, let him look back at the story. Note his ability to scan to find the answer.

MEETING INDIVIDUAL NEEDS

If S. needs more practice in blending sounds, use small flash cards with a single letter, digraph, or beginning blend on each card. (Use only the short vowels studied so far: *i, u, e, a*.)

1. Put together a vowel and ending consonant, such as *at*. Substitute different beginning letters, and have S. read the rhyming words, such as: *cat, fat, that*.
2. Put together a beginning consonant and a vowel, such as *ba*. Substitute different ending letters, and have S. read the words, such as: *bad, bat, back, bag, bath*. (Avoid using *r* after the vowel.)

In *More Stories 2*, the stories for Lesson 7 may be read in class or suggested for reading at home.

Practices 8A–8E in *Focus on Phonics 2* may be used after Lesson 8. Or, you may prefer to save all of the short *a* practices to use as a review after Lesson 9.

OBJECTIVES

To help your student:

- identify the vowel *a* and its short sound /a/.
- recognize the consonant blends *gr* as in *grass* and *gl* as in *glass* and the ending blend *nch* as in *lunch*.
- read the following new words:
  Chart words: *path, grass, glass, half, laugh, factory*
  Story words: *after, lunch.*
- read a story, using the new chart and story words.
- summarize a story by listing the main events in the order in which they happened.
- scan a story to find a certain paragraph.
- review dropping final silent *e* before adding *-ing*.
- contrast the vowel sounds /a/, /e/, /i/, /u/.
- write the new chart and story words.

INTRODUCTION

T: In this lesson, you will read some more words with the vowel sound /a/. In the story, you will read more about Jack and Ann.

I. Reading

CHART: Page 46

Title and key word. Have S. read the lesson title, name of vowel, and key word. Have him give the short sound for the vowel: /a/.

Lines 1–6. Tell S. that the first three words in the chart are pronounced the way they are written, but the other three words are not pronounced just the way they are written. He will need to look at column 3 for help in pronouncing them. Have him study the chart and read the words to himself. When he has finished, have him read each word aloud. Call his attention to these points:

1. The sound for *th* in *path*. The sound is /th/ as in *think* and *with*.
2. The *gr* blend at the beginning of *grass*. Have S. listen for the two consonant sounds /gr/ at the beginning of the word and tell the names of the letters.

   Double *s* at the end of *grass*.
3. The *gl* blend at the beginning of *glass*. Have S. listen for the two consonant sounds /gl/ and tell the names of the letters.

   Double *s* at the end of *glass*. Also, point out that *grass* and *glass* rhyme.
4. The silent *l* in *half*.

5. The silent *u* in *laugh* and the sound /f/ for *gh*.
6. The sound for *or* in factory is /er/. You hear /er/ but must remember that in this word it is written *or*.

   At the end of *factory*, *y* is a vowel and has the same sound as in *city*.

Review. Have S. read all of the words again, going down the last column of the chart.

STORY: Page 47 (Lunch on the Grass)

Have S. read the title of the story and the new words.

Silent reading and summarizing. Ask S. to read the whole story to himself. Then have him summarize by telling the main events in the order in which they happened. His summary might be similar to the following:

1. Ann and Jack visit the glass factory.
2. They have lunch on the grass in back of the factory.
3. Ann gives Jack half of her apple.
4. After lunch, they run on the path and laugh.

Scanning. Ask S. how many paragraphs are in the story [six]. Have him scan the story to find each of the paragraphs described below. Tell him to look through the story quickly to find the paragraph you describe. Explain that he should not read each word, but should let his eyes go quickly down the page to find that paragraph.

After he finds each paragraph, have him read it aloud to verify that it is right.

Ask S. to find the paragraph that tells:

—about Ann giving Jack half of the apple [par.4].
—where they have lunch [par. 2].
—what they do after lunch [par. 5].
—what they visited [par. 1].
—what they do while they run [par. 6].

Oral reading. Have S. read the whole story aloud.

Reading between the lines. Discuss these questions.

1. Did Ann and Jack visit the glass factory in the morning or in the afternoon? How do you know? [In the morning. They had lunch after the visit.]
2. Do you think Ann and Jack had a good time?
3. Does the story tell *why* they visited the glass factory? [No.] (Mention to S. that later he will read more about Jack and the glass factory.)
4. What are some factories in your area? What products do they make? Do any of these factories give tours for visitors?

II. Skills Practice

T: Please close your book. We will have some practice on listening for vowel sounds and consonant blends. We will also have an exercise on the *-ing* ending.

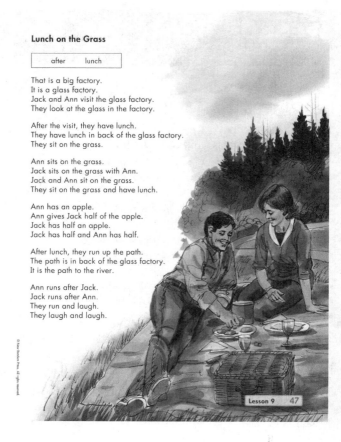

PRACTICE 1: Vowel Sounds /a/, /e/, /i/, /u/

Write the letters *a, e, i, u* on the board. Tell S. that these are the vowels he has studied so far in this book. Have him give the name and short sound for each.

Write the key words *apple, egg, in, up* on the board, and have S. read them.

T: I will say three words. Which word on the board has the same vowel sound as the words I say:

Ed, red, let? [S: egg.]   *fun, mud, duck?* [S: up.]
am, an, pan? [S: apple.]   *brick, it, till?*   [S: in.]

Point to each key word, and ask S. to think of another word with the same vowel sound.

PRACTICE 2: Beginning Consonant Blends *gr, gl*

Write *grass* and *glass* on the board. Have S. read the words and tell what consonant blend each word begins with. As he answers, underline the blends *gr* and *gl*.

T: I will say two words.
Which word starts with the blend *gr* as in *grass*:

grip, rip?   *gate, great?*   *gave, grave?*
ray, gray?   *grain, gain?*   *ground, round?*

T: This time, listen for the blend *gl*.
Which word starts with blend *gl* as in *glass*:

Glenn, get?   *love, glove?*   *glad, grade?*
low, glow?   *glue, goo?*   *grow, glow?*

PRACTICE 3: Ending Consonant Blend *nch*

T: (Write *lunch* on the board.) Read the word. [S: lunch.] *Lunch* ends with the consonant blend *nch*. (Underline *nch*.) The sound /n/ is blended with the sound /ch/. Read the word again, please. [S: lunch.]

T: Which word ends with the *nch* blend as in *lunch*:
ran, ranch?   *bench, Ben?*   *bun, bunch?*
in, inch?   *pitch, pinch?*   *itch, inch?*

PRACTICE 4: Dropping Final Silent *e* Before *-ing*

Write *have* on the board, and have S. read it.

T: What will the word be if you add the ending *-ing*? [S: having.] What letter is left off *have* before *-ing* is added? [S: e.] Say the letters in *having*. [S: h-a-v-i-n-g.] (Write *having* by *have*.)

In the same way, have S. add *-ing* to *come, give, live*. (This is a review.)

48   Lesson 9

III. Writing

CHECK HOMEWORK: Page 45

Check this page with S. Have him correct any errors.

CHECKUP: Page 48

Have S. read the title and directions. Then have him do the page. Check his work, and have him correct any errors. To help him correct errors, refer him back to the chart where the word first appeared.

As you go over the last item, *basket,* point out that *k* is used for the sound /k/ before the letter *e.*

WRITING LESSON: Page 49

Study. Help S. study and write these words: (1) *half,* (2) *laugh,* (3) *factory,* (4) *have.* Call attention to the same points as you did when teaching the chart. For *factory,* point out also that the sound /k/ is written with *c* before a consonant.

Listen and write. Dictate these words for S. to write: (1) *glass,* (2) *grass,* (3) *path,* (4) *after.* Check his work, and have him correct any errors by erasing the whole word and writing it over.

Then have him cover the top half of the page. Dictate these sentences for him to write:

1. Ann sits on the grass.
2. It is a glass factory.
3. Ann runs after Jack.
4. Jack has half an apple.
5. Jack and Ann laugh.

Go over the sentences with S., giving careful attention to capitals and periods as well as spelling. Call attention to the spelling of *and, Ann,* and *an,* and discuss what each word means. Review the use of *an* before a word beginning with a vowel sound, such as *an apple, an egg, an olive.*

Have S. correct any errors. Praise him for what he has done well. Encourage him if he is having difficulty.

HOMEWORK: Pages 50–51

Have S. read the directions on page 50. Explain that for each exercise, there is a question and answer. He is to read the question and fill in the missing word in the answer. He can find the missing word in the question.

Ask S. to read number 3 and tell you the missing words. If he gives the word *she* for the first blank, tell him that is correct, but for this exercise you would like for him to use the same word that is in the question. For this answer, he will write *Ann.* Follow the same procedure for number 5, in which he might use *he* instead of *Jack.*

Have S. read the directions on page 51. Ask him to study the chart and read the story at home and to practice any words he missed in the Writing Lesson.

CHECKING PROGRESS

Vowels and digraphs. The Checkup on page 44 will help you determine if S. can distinguish the vowel sounds /a/, /e/, /i/, /u/, and the sounds /wh/, /th/, /ng/, which are written with digraphs. If he had difficulty with any of these, plan additional exercises for practice.

Consonant blends. You may want to check your student's progress in recognizing consonant blends. Make a flash card for each of these words: *bring, stand, truck, twelve, friend, black, Smith, grass, glass.* Have S. read each word and give the two sounds that are in the consonant blend. Example: [S: bring, /br/.]

Say each of the following words, and have S. name the consonant blend: *blot, stack, smog, grin, glad, frog, twin, trick, brim.* Example: T: *blot.* [S: *bl.*]

Punctuation. Ask S. to read each of the following selections, and note his observation of punctuation marks. (It will help to write each selection on a separate slip of paper or card.)

> Dan yells, "A rat! A rat!"
> Is Fred very sick?
> No, he is not very sick.
> Fred says, "Are the eggs fresh?"
> Ellen says, "Yes, the eggs are very fresh."
> Do you live in the city?

Have S. point out the punctuation marks in each selection.

MEETING INDIVIDUAL NEEDS

Practice in word recognition. Make a flash card for each new chart and story word in Lessons 6–8. (See Lesson 1 for the way to make these cards.) Follow the suggestions in Lesson 1, under the section called Checking Progress, for using them.

Practice in fluent reading. S. should be learning to recognize a short phrase at a glance. You may find it helpful to have him read some phrase cards. Flash the card fairly quickly, so that he must make a quick response. Also, note his accuracy in reading. You may write some of the following phrases on cards:

at the factory	in back of	in the valley
on the grass	in the city	in the kitchen
in the glass	to the boys	with his sister
up the path	for the fish	to her family

Reading practice. In *More Stories 2,* the stories for Lesson 8 may be read in class or suggested for reading at home.

Phonics practice. Practices 9A–9H in *Focus on Phonics 2* may be used after Lesson 9. Or, if you have saved all of the short *a* practices to use as a review, you may do them now. Another possibility is to save all of *Focus on Phonics 2* to use after completing book 2.

Fill in the letters.

 g u n   h e ns

 duc k   ri n g

 l i l y   be l l

 r a t   wh istle

 k itchen   mo t h er

 fun n y   bas k et

Study.

1. half   3. factory

2. laugh   4. have

Listen and write.

1. glass   3. path

2. grass   4. after

Listen and write.

1. Ann sits on the grass.

2. It is a glass factory.

3. Ann runs after Jack.

4. Jack has half an apple.

5. Jack and Ann laugh.

Fill in the words.

1. Is that a glass factory?

  Yes, that is a **glass** factory.

2. Is the factory little?

  No, the **factory** is big.

3. Does Ann sit on the grass?

  Yes, **Ann** sits on the **grass**.

4. Do Jack and Ann have dinner?

  No, they **have** lunch.

5. Does Jack run after Ann?

  Yes, **Jack** runs **after** Ann.

Fill in the letters.

 f a ctory   pa t h

 gla s s   gr a ss

Fill in the words.

1. Jack and Ann visit the

  big **glass** factory.

2. Ann sits on the **grass**.

3. Jack has **half** an apple.

4. They run up the **path**.

5. They run and **laugh**.

OBJECTIVES

To help your student:

- recognize the vowel *o* and its associated short sound /o/ as in *olive*.
- recognize the abbreviation *Dr.* for *Doctor*.
- recognize the consonant blends *cl* as in *clock* and *dr* as in *drop*.
- observe the use of *c* for the sound /k/ before a consonant, as in *clock* and *doctor*.
- review the use of *ck* for the sound /k/ at the end of a word, following a short vowel sound, as in *rock*.
- recognize rhyming words such as *not* and *got*, *stop* and *top*, *rock* and *lock*.
- recognize that *-ed* is a word ending.
- read the following new words in two charts and stories:
  Chart words: *doctor, Dr., office, hot, shot, doll, Molly*
  Story words: *got, Chan, head*
  Chart words: *rock, lock, clock, top, stops, stopped, dollar*
  Story words: *Don, Tom, John, job, fix, dropped.*
- read two stories, using the new chart and story words.
- scan a story to find a certain paragraph.
- recognize the motivation of a character in a story.
- review the following punctuation marks: period, comma, question mark, quotation marks.
- recognize and read direct quotations.
- review the endings *-s, -'s, -ing*.
- write the new chart and story words.

INTRODUCTION

T: Today's lesson is about another vowel sound. Please turn to page 52 and find out what it is.

I. Reading

CHART: Page 52

Title and key word. Have S. read the lesson title, name of vowel, and key word. Have him give the short sound for the vowel: /o/.

Line 1

T: Look at the first picture. Then look at the top word in the next column. (Point to *doctor*.) Look at the way it is written in the next column. What is the word? [S: doctor.]

T: Sometimes we use an abbreviation for *doctor*. The abbreviation is written in the second column, under the word *doctor*. (Point to *Dr*.) What kind of *d* is used? [S: Capital.] That is because it is a title. Remember,

we use a capital letter for the titles *Mr.* and *Mrs.* We use the abbreviation *Dr.* only when it is followed by the doctor's name.

T: (Point to column 4.) Read the word again. [S: doctor.] What is the abbreviation? [S: *Dr.*]

Line 2. Have S. look at the picture and word (*office*) and refer to column 3 for help in sounding it out. Call attention to the silent *e*, the sound /s/ for *c*, and the double *f*. Have S. read the word again in column 4.

Note: If S. pronounces the *o* in *office* as /aw/, let him do so. Explain that in some parts of the country, it is pronounced /o/ as in *olive*.

Lines 3–6. Tell S. that the other words in the chart are pronounced the way they are written. Have him study the chart and read the words to himself. When he has finished, have him read each word aloud. Then ask these questions.

1. Which word rhymes with *hot*? [S: shot.]
2. In *hot*, what vowel sound comes before the /t/ sound? [S: /o/.] Remember, when words end with the same vowel and consonant sound combination, they rhyme. The combination in these words is /ot/. Can you think of a word not on the chart that rhymes with *hot* and *shot*? [Possible answers: *cot, dot, got, lot, not, rot, spot*.]
3. What is the double consonant in *doll* and *Molly*? [S: *l*.]
4. What kind of sound does *y* have at the end of *Molly*? [S: A vowel sound.]

Review. Have S. read all of the words again, going down the last column of the chart.

STORY: Page 53 (At the Doctor's Office)

Have S. read the story title and the new words. Call attention to the silent *a* in *head*.

Directed silent reading and discussion. Ask S. to read the whole story to himself to find out why Mrs. Roberts took Molly to the doctor. Also, he should find out what the doctor did for Molly. When he has finished, ask these questions:

1. Why did Mrs. Roberts take Molly to the doctor? [Because Molly was sick. Her head was hot.]
2. What did Dr. Chan do for Molly?
   [She gave Molly a shot.]
3. What did Molly tell the doctor?
   [She told the doctor that her doll was sick.]
4. What did the doctor do before giving Molly a shot? [She gave the doll a shot.] Do you think the doctor *really* gave the doll a shot or just pretended to? [She just pretended.] Why do you think she gave the doll a shot? [So that Molly wouldn't be afraid.]
5. Did Molly get well? [Yes, she got well very quickly.]

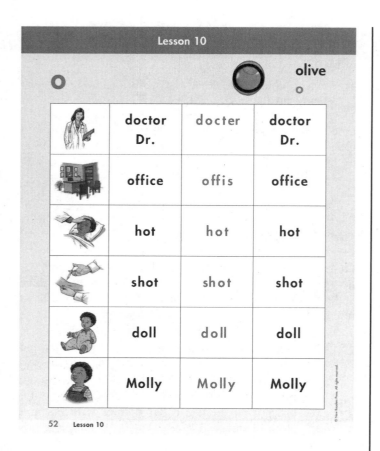

o   olive
              o

	doctor Dr.	docter	doctor Dr.
	office	offis	office
	hot	hot	hot
	shot	shot	shot
	doll	doll	doll
	Molly	Molly	Molly

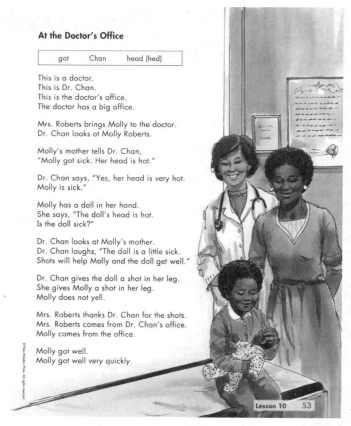

At the Doctor's Office

got	Chan	head (hed)

This is a doctor.
This is Dr. Chan.
This is the doctor's office.
The doctor has a big office.

Mrs. Roberts brings Molly to the doctor.
Dr. Chan looks at Molly Roberts.

Molly's mother tells Dr. Chan,
"Molly got sick. Her head is hot."

Dr. Chan says, "Yes, her head is very hot.
Molly is sick."

Molly has a doll in her hand.
She says, "The doll's head is hot.
Is the doll sick?"

Dr. Chan looks at Molly's mother.
Dr. Chan laughs, "The doll is a little sick.
Shots will help Molly and the doll get well."

Dr. Chan gives the doll a shot in her leg.
She gives Molly a shot in her leg.
Molly does not yell.

Mrs. Roberts thanks Dr. Chan for the shots.
Mrs. Roberts comes from Dr. Chan's office.
Molly comes from the office.

Molly got well.
Molly got well very quickly.

Word study. Have S. find each of the new story words in the story. Ask him to find two words in the story that rhyme with *hot* and *shot* [*got, not*].

Ask S. to find the words that end with -'s and read them [*doctor's, Molly's, doll's*].

Punctuation review. Have S. find each of these punctuation marks: period, comma, question mark, quotation marks.

Oral reading. In paragraph 3, have S. find the part that Molly's mother says and read it aloud. Have him do the same thing for what Dr. Chan says in paragraphs 4 and 6, and for what Molly says in paragraph 5.

Then have S. read the whole story aloud. Encourage him to read with expression and observe punctuation marks.

Relating the story to everyday life. Discuss some of these points with S.

1. How can we help to prepare a child for a visit to the doctor or for an operation?

2. Why do people sometimes put off visits to the doctor?

3. Why is it important to find a regular clinic or doctor to go to *before* you get sick?

In your discussion, talk about the need for communication between patient and doctor. We need to know how to ask questions about our health. If we need treatment, we need to know what will be done. Both adults and children need reassurance and answers to their questions.

CHART: Page 54

Explain that, in this lesson, there are two charts about the vowel *o*. Have S. read the name of the vowel and key word. Have him give the short sound for the vowel.

Lines 1–6. Tell S. that most of the words in this chart are pronounced the way they are written. Have him study the chart and read the words to himself. When he has finished, have him read each word aloud. Then ask these questions:

1. Which words rhyme with *rock*? [S: lock, clock.]

2. What is the consonant sound at the end of *rock, lock,* and *clock*? [S: /k/.] How is it written? [S: *ck.*] What is the sound before the /k/ sound? [S: /o/.] Remember, when /k/ follows a short vowel sound, it is usually written with *ck.*

3. How many consonant sounds do you hear before the vowel sound in *clock*? [S: Two.] What are the names of the consonants? [S: *cl.*] This is another consonant blend. We call it the *cl* blend.

   Say the word again, and listen for the consonant blend. [S: clock.] Say the two sounds that make the blend. [S: /kl/.] When the sound /k/ is followed by a consonant sound, it is almost always written with *c.*

4. What other word in the chart begins with a consonant blend? [S: stops.] What is the blend? [S: *st.*]

5. If you leave the *-s* ending off *stops*, what is the word? [S: stop.] What word in the chart does *stop* rhyme with? [S: top.]

6. Which words have double consonants? [S: stopped, dollar.] (For *stopped*, also explain that *-ed* is another word ending. In the word *stopped*, it is pronounced /t/.)

Review. Have S. read all of the words again, going down the last column of the chart.

STORY: Page 55 (John Oliver's Shop)

Have S. read the story title and the new words. Call attention to the capital letters in the names and also the silent *h* in *John*. For *dropped*, point out that the *-ed* ending in this word is pronounced /t/, the same as in *stopped*.

Directed silent reading. Ask S. to read the whole story to himself to find out who comes to John's shop and what jobs these people ask him to do. When he has finished, ask these questions:

1. Who comes to the shop? [Tom Bell, Don Roberts, and Ann Smith.]

2. What does Tom want to have fixed? [His clock.] What happened to his clock? [He dropped it.] How much will John charge to fix it? [Five dollars.]

3. What does Don want to have fixed? [His lock.] What happened to his lock? [He dropped it on a rock.] How much will John charge to fix it? [One dollar.]

4. What does Ann want to have fixed? [Her box.] What happened to her box? [She dropped it on a rock.] How much will John charge to fix it? [Two dollars.]

Word study. Have S. read each of the new story words and find it in the story. Then ask him to find the full name of each person in the story and read it.

Have S. find the word *funny* in paragraph 7. Ask him to read the paragraph aloud and tell what he thinks the word *funny* means here [odd or strange]. Ask S. *why* John said "That is funny" when Ann told him what happened to her box. [Two people in a row told John about having the same kind of accident.]

Scanning and oral reading. Have S. scan the story to find each paragraph described below. When he finds it, have him read the paragraph aloud.

Ask S. to find the paragraph that tells:
— what Don wants John to fix [par. 4].
— what John will charge to fix the clock [par. 3].
— what happened to Tom's clock [par. 2].
— what John does in his shop [par. 1].
— what Ann dropped [par. 6].

Have S. read the whole story aloud. Or, you may read the part of John and have S. read the parts of the people who come to the shop. Then reverse parts. Encourage S. to observe punctuation marks and read with expression.

Reading between the lines. Ask these questions:

1. Which repair job cost the most? [Tom's clock.]

2. How much money will John get for the three repair jobs? [Eight dollars.]

3. What do *you* do when things you own get broken?

Relating the story to everyday life. Show S. how *five dollars* can be written as $5. Write other prices with the dollar sign for him to read, such as $1, $2, $10.

II. Skills Practice

T: Please close your book. We will have some exercises on listening for consonant blends and rhyming words and on adding some endings to words.

PRACTICE 1: Beginning Consonant Blends *cl, dr, st*

Write the blends *cl, dr, st* on the board, and have S. read them.

T: Which word begins with the *cl* blend as in *clock:*

lip, clip?	*cap, clap?*	*clean, green?*
cloud, loud?	*club, cub?*	*class, glass?*

T: Which word begins with the *dr* blend as in *drop:*

rag, drag?	*dress, desk?*	*drink, bring?*
drain, rain?	*try, dry?*	*cream, dream?*

T: Which word begins with the *st* blend as in *stuck:*

top, stop?	*drop, story?*	*study, clock?*
sand, stand?	*stop, shop?*	*Smith, stand?*

Lesson 10   53

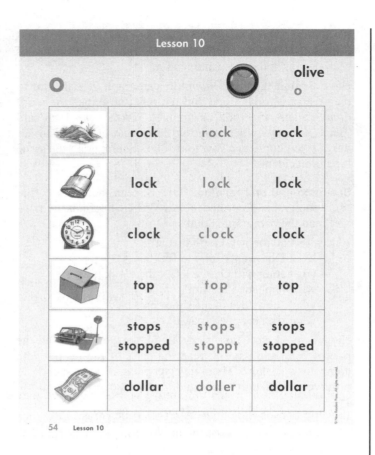

PRACTICE 2: Rhyming Words with the Vowel Sound /o/

Write *hot, top, rock,* and have S. read these words.

T: I will say two words. Which word rhymes with *hot:*
   got, cat?   not, net?   let, lot?   not, nut?

T: Which word rhymes with *top:*
   ship, shop?   mop, map?   cup, cop?   drop, drip?

T: Which word rhymes with *rock:*
   sock, sick?   deck, dock?   luck, lock?   black, clock?

PRACTICE 3: Noun Endings -s and -'s

Write *doll* on the board. Have S. read it and tell how we can make it mean more than one [add *-s*]. As he answers, write *dolls* by *doll.*

Ask S. to name the other new words in Lesson 10 to which we can add *-s* to mean more than one. List the words as S. says them: *rock, lock, clock, top, dollar, job, doctor, office, shot, head.* Then have him say what each word would be with the ending *-s.*

Write *Molly's, doll's, doctor's, Oliver's* on the board. Have S. read the words, tell what the ending is [*-'s*], and what it means [belongs to]. Then ask S. to read each word and tell something that might belong to that person, such as *Molly's doll.* [Possible answers: *Molly's mother, doll's*

head, doctor's office, Oliver's shop, or other answers if usage is correct.]

PRACTICE 4: Verb Endings -s and -ing

Tell S. that he has learned several action words to which we can add the ending *-s* or the ending *-ing.* Write *stop,* and have S. read it. Ask him to add *-s* to *stop* and say the word. Then ask him to add *-ing* to *stop* and say the word. (As this is an oral practice, there is no need to call attention to the doubling of *p* in *stopping.*)

Follow the same procedure with these words: *look, laugh, yell, come, thank, drop, bring, give.* Write each word, and have S. read it. Then have him tell what it would be with *-s* and with *-ing.*

III. Writing

CHECK HOMEWORK: Pages 50–51

Check these pages with S., and have him correct any errors. On page 46, if he forgot and used the pronouns *she* in number 3 and *he* in number 5, accept these as correct answers even though you asked him to use the names *Ann* and *Jack.* But, ask him what name *she* stands for and what name *he* stands for in the answers.

WRITING LESSON: Page 56

Study. Help S. study and write the words listed below. Call attention to these points:

1. *doctor.* The letter *c* is used for the sound /k/. Remind S. that /k/ followed by a consonant sound is usually written with *c*. The sound /er/ at the end is written *or*.
2. *office.* Point out the double *f*, the letter *c* for /s/, and the silent *e* at the end.
3. *dollar.* Point out the double *l*. The sound /er/ at the end is written *ar*.
4. *stopped.* Point out the double *p* and the use of *ed* for the sound /t/.
5. *dropped.* Point out the consonant blend *dr*, the double *p*, and the *ed* for the sound /t/. Also, mention that *dropped* and *stopped* rhyme.
6. *John.* Point out the capital *J* and silent *h*.

Listen and write. Dictate these words for S. to write:

(1) *hot*, (2) *got*, (3) *shot*, (4) *top*, (5) *stop*, (6) *drop*, (7) *rock*, (8) *clock*. Check his work, and have him correct any errors.

Then have him cover the top half of the page. Dictate these sentences for him to write:

1. John can fix that lock.
2. Is the doll sick?

Check his work. If he didn't make the question mark, have him do so. Ask him to correct any errors.

HOMEWORK: Page 57

Go over the directions with S. Ask him to read both charts and stories in Lesson 10 again at home.

CHECKING PROGRESS

Check your student's progress in oral reading by having him read a paragraph from each story in Lessons 8–9. Record the number of errors for each of the following:

1. Observation of punctuation marks.
2. Omission of words.
3. Substitution of words.
4. Repetition of words.
5. Doesn't know a word.

If S. makes more than three errors in a paragraph, have him read a paragraph from an earlier lesson. Try to find a paragraph that he can read with no more than one or two errors. When you find a paragraph on his level of oral reading, make note of it.

You may check your student's progress in comprehension skills by having him read new material using old words. A good selection for this is the story "The Man on the Path," one of the three stories for Lesson 9 in *More Stories 2*.

Have S. read the first two pages of this story silently and then answer these questions:

1. What does Jack King think of when he is in bed? [His glass factory.]
2. How long does he think about this? [An hour.]
3. Why does he get up? [He decides to go to the factory.]
4. What will he do at the factory? [Write letters.]
5. What does he see on the path? [Some glass.]
6. What does he see when he looks up the path? [A man.]
7. What does Jack think when he sees the man? [Is he a bad man?]
8. What makes Jack think this might be a bad man? [It is late at night. The workers are not at the factory. Jack has seen some glass on the path.]

S. should be able to answer six of these questions accurately. If he doesn't remember an answer, let him look back at the story. Notice his ability to scan a page to find the right answer.

MEETING INDIVIDUAL NEEDS

Oral reading. If S. needs to improve oral reading, you may find some of the following suggestions helpful:

1. Choose a paragraph on his level of reading, and have S. read it aloud *with* you.

2. If you have a tape recorder, have S. read aloud while you record him. Play back the tape, and let S. hear himself reading. He will be able to detect some of his own errors. (Do this only if S. is interested and will not be discouraged if he makes errors.) Erase the tape after S. has listened to let him know that you will not play it for anyone else. Or, if he wishes, you can keep the tape and make another recording of the same paragraph later to show his improvement.

3. Make some recordings of your own reading of some paragraphs in earlier lessons. Lend these tapes and a player to S. Ask him to practice reading the same paragraph aloud as he listens to you read it on the tape.

4. If your student's problems in oral reading are mainly in word recognition, give extra practice with flash cards in class.

Vowel sounds. If S. needs practice in distinguishing vowel sounds, these two exercises may be helpful:

1. Mix up flash cards for the new chart and story in Lessons 8–10 along with some words from previous lessons. (For this exercise, omit any words that end with *y*.) Ask S. to sort the cards into piles according to the vowel sound in the word: /a/, /e/, /i/, /o/, or /u/. He should sort the cards by the *sound* of the vowel, not by its name.

Study.

1. doctor   4. stopped

2. office   5. dropped

3. dollar   6. John

Listen and write.

1. hot   5. stop

2. got   6. drop

3. shot   7. rock

4. top   8. clock

Listen and write.

1. John can fix that lock.

2. Is the doll sick?

Fill in the letters.

clock   duck

lock   doll

stops   doctor

Fill in the words.

1. The doctor is in her office.

2. Molly's head is hot.

3. Don dropped his lock.

4. John will fix Tom's clock for five dollars.

2. Make a small flash card for each of these vowels: *a, e, i, o, u*. Then make a second set of cards, leaving a blank for the missing vowel in these words:

c __ t	st __ p	b __ t
m __ d	D __ n	h __ t
f __ x	sh __ t	l __ ck

Working with one word card at a time, dictate different words that can be formed with different vowels. Have S. select the vowel card to match the word you say, put it in the blank, and then read the word. These are the words you can dictate:

cat, cut	stop, step	bat, bet, bit
mud, mad	Don, Dan	hit, hot, hat
fix, fox	shot, shut	lock, luck, lick

Reading practice. In *More Stories 2*, the stories for Lesson 9 may be read in class or suggested for reading at home. (If you started the story "The Man on the Path" as suggested in Checking Progress, you should provide an opportunity for S. to finish reading it.)

Phonics practice. Practices 10A–10C in *Focus on Phonics 2* may be used after Lesson 10.

Supplementary lesson. If you think that S. needs a review of the short vowel sounds before going on to the *r*-controlled vowel sounds in Lessons 11–12, you may want to plan a supplementary lesson for next time. This will also allow more time for S. to practice writing and spelling skills as well as reading skills.

You may use any suggestions in this lesson or previous lessons that are suitable. You may also want to use the practices in *Focus on Phonics 2* that contrast short vowels if S. has not already done them.

OBJECTIVES

To help your student:

- recognize the sound /er/ and the three ways it is written: *er, ir, ur*.
- recognize the consonant blend *sk* as in *skirt*.
- review the short vowel sounds: /a/, /e/, /i/, /o/, /u/, and the vowel sound /y/ as in *lily*.
- recognize the ending *-ed* and the three ways it is pronounced: /d/ as in *yelled*, /t/ as in *picked*, and /ed/ as in *hunted*.
- read the following new words:

  Chart words: *burn, fern, father, were, skirt, curtains, burning, burned*
  Story words: *rug, ran, picked, yelled, was, heard, match, Miller, yelling, running*
  Chart words: *hurry, hurried, nurse, person, cover, covered, better, first*
  Story words: *us, then, burns, said, helping, looked*.

- read a longer story, in two parts, using the new chart and story words.
- recognize the cause and effect of events in the story.
- review the ending *-ing*.
- write the new chart and story words.

INTRODUCTION

T: You have studied each of the short vowel sounds. You have learned the name of the letter that stands for each sound. In today's lesson, you will study another sound. This sound is written in three ways.

I. Reading

CHART: Page 58

Title and key word. Have S. read the lesson title.

T: Look at the letters in the top right-hand corner. What are the first two letters? [S: er.] What sound did you learn for these letters in the word *sister*? [S: /er/.] There are some other letters that stand for the sound /er/. What are the two letters under *er*? [S: ir.] What are the two letters under *ir*? [S: ur.] *Er, ur,* and *ir* all stand for the sound /er/.

T: Look at the three words at the top of the page. What is the first word? [S: her.] What letters stand for the sound /er/ in *her*? [S: er.]

T: What is the next word? [S: girl.] What letters stand for the sound /er/ in *girl*? [S: ir.]

T: The next word is a new word, but you can sound it out. What is it? [S: burn.] What letters stand for the sound /er/ in *burn*? [S: ur.]

T: Whenever you see *er, ir,* or *ur,* you will know that it stands for the sound /er/.

Line 1. Have S. look at the first picture and read *fern*.

T: A fern is a plant, but the word is also used for a woman's name. In the story, you will find it as a girl's name. When *Fern* is used as a name, what kind of *f* will it have? [S: Capital.] What letters stand for the sound /er/ in *fern*? [S: er.]

Have S. read the word again in column 4.

Lines 2–3. Teach in the usual manner. In each word, call attention to the sound /er/ and how it is written. In *father*, point out that the sound /o/ is written with *a*. In *were*, point out the silent *e* at the end.

Line 4. Have S. look at the picture, read *skirt*, and tell what letters stand for the sound /er/.

T: How many consonant sounds do you hear before the /er/ sound? [S: Two.] What are they? [S: /sk/.] This is another consonant blend. We call it the *sk* blend.

Have S. read the word again in column 4.

Line 5. Teach in the usual manner, having S. look at column 3 for help in sounding out *curtains*. Ask what letters stand for the sound /er/. Point out that *ai* sounds like /u/ in *curtains*.

Line 6. Have S. look at the last picture.

T: There are two words next to the picture. Look at the top word. What is it? [S: burning.] What is the ending in *burning?* [S: -ing.] What is the word without the ending? [S: burn.] *Burn* is one of the words at the top of the page. (Point to it.)

T: Look at the word under *burning*. This word has the ending *-ed*. Look at column 3 to find out how to pronounce it. What is the word? [S: burned.] In *burned*, the ending *-ed* is pronounced /d/. What letters stand for the sound /er/ in *burned?* [S: ur.]

Have S. read both words again in column 4.

Review. Have S. read the three key words and all of the words in the last column of the chart again.

STORY: Page 59 (Fern Gets Burned)

Have S. read the title and new words. Call attention to these points in the new words:

1. The sound /er/ in *Miller* and how it is written.
2. The *-ing* ending in *yelling* and *running*, and the root words *yell* and *run* (the root words are old words).
3. The *-ed* ending in *picked* and *yelled*, and the root words *pick* and *yell* (old words).

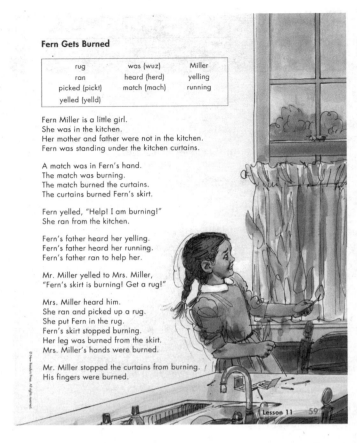

Directed silent reading and discussion. Ask S. to read the whole page silently to find out how Fern got burned.

When he has finished, ask the questions below to check his comprehension. Encourage S. to answer in his own words, without referring to the book, as much as possible, instead of answering by reading sentences from the story aloud. This will help you know whether he has really understood what he has read. If S. can't remember a fact, however, let him look at the book.

Accept any answers that express essentially the same thought as in the suggested answers here.

1. How did the fire start? [Fern was playing with matches in the kitchen and accidentally set the curtains on fire.]

2. How did Fern's skirt catch on fire? [The curtains burned her skirt.]

3. How did Fern react when her skirt started burning? [She yelled and ran out of the kitchen.]

4. How did Mrs. Miller save Fern? [She wrapped Fern in a rug to stop her skirt from burning.]

5. What kept the Millers' home from burning up? [Mr. Miller stopped the curtains from burning.]

6. How did Fern's leg get burned? [It got burned when her skirt caught on fire.]

7. How did Mrs. Miller's hands get burned? [They got burned when she put out the fire in Fern's skirt.]

8. How did Mr. Miller's fingers get burned? [They got burned when he put out the fire in the curtains.]

CHART: Page 60

T: Here is another chart for the sound /er/. What are the three ways that the sound /er/ can be written? (Point to letters at top right.) [S: *er, ir, ur*.]

Have S. read each key word at the top and tell how the sound /er/ is written in the word.

Lines 1–6. Help S. study the chart, going through it with him line by line. Call his attention to these points:

1. The way the sound /er/ is written in each word.
2. The final *y* as a vowel in *hurry*.
3. The ending *-ed* in *hurried* and *covered*, and the way it is pronounced /d/.

Review. Have S. read the three key words and all of the words in the last column of the chart again.

STORY: Page 61 (Hurry to the Doctor!)

Explain that this page continues the story "Fern Gets Burned." Review the first part by asking who set the fire and who got burned.

Have S. read the new words. Call his attention to the *-ing* ending in *helping* and the root word *help* (an old word). Also call his attention to the *-ed* ending in *looked*, the way it is pronounced /t/, and the root word *look* (an old word).

Directed silent reading and discussion. Ask S. to read the whole page silently to find out what happened to the three burned persons. When he has finished, have him summarize what happened in his own words. Then ask these questions to check his comprehension further:

1. Who was the first person the Millers saw when they got to the doctor's office? [The nurse.]
2. Did the Millers have to wait, or did the nurse get the doctor right away? [The nurse got the doctor right away.]
3. Which person's burns were treated first? [Fern's.]
4. Did Dr. Chan or the nurse cover Fern's burns? [Dr. Chan did.]
5. Did Dr. Chan cover Mr. and Mrs. Miller's burns herself, or did she tell the nurse what to do? [She told the nurse what to do.]

Oral reading. Have S. read the whole story (pages 59 and 61) aloud. Encourage him to observe punctuation marks and to read with expression.

Reading between the lines. Discuss these questions:

1. Mr. Miller let his wife save Fern while he went into the kitchen and stopped the curtains from burning. What does that show about him? [He knew how to act fast. He had confidence in his wife.]
2. Why do you think the Millers were able to see the doctor without waiting? [The nurse must have seen that their burns were serious.]
3. Why do you think Fern was treated first? [Because she was a child. Her burns may have been worse.]

Relating the story to everyday life. In discussing these questions with S., give him a chance to tell what he knows. Bring out any information that he doesn't know or doesn't think of.

1. How might this fire have been prevented? (Mention teaching children not to play with matches and keeping matches and lighters out of their reach.)
2. Why was running a bad thing for Fern to do when her skirt caught on fire? (Explain that when a person's clothing is on fire, running makes the fire burn more.)
3. When a person's clothing is burning, what is the best way to put out the fire? (Explain that fire needs air to burn. Wrapping the person in a rug, blanket, coat, or heavy towels will smother the fire.)
4. What is the emergency number to call in your area to report a fire?
5. What are some things you can do to be prepared in case of fire? (Some things that might be mentioned are smoke detectors, fire extinguishers, teaching children what to do, having fire drills with the family, keeping emergency numbers where you can find them quickly. You may want to emphasize that fire departments warn us not to try to put out a fire by ourselves unless it is *very* small. Usually, it's best to get everyone outside and phone from somewhere else.)

II. Skills Practice

T: Please close your book. We will have some exercises on listening for vowel sounds and a new consonant blend. We will also practice adding endings to words.

PRACTICE 1: Review of Vowel Sounds

Write *a, e, i, o, u, y*. Tell S. these are the vowels he has studied. Have him give the name and sound for each letter (the short vowel sound for *a, e, i, o, u* and the vowel sound for *y* as in *lily*).

T: What is the vowel sound in these words:

rug, run?	*then, leg?*	*us, gun?*	*that, Jack?*
pick, fix?	*has, Chan?*	*Ed, yes?*	*rock, top?*

T: What vowel sound do you hear at the end of these words: *hurry, funny?* [S: /y/.] What letter stands for the sound? [S: *y*.]

T: Now I'll say two other words. Which one ends with *y: happy, yelling?* [S: happy.]

PRACTICE 2: Beginning Consonant Blend *sk*

T: (Write *sk* on the board.) This is the blend that *skirt* begins with. What are the names of the letters in the blend? [S: *sk*.]

T: Which word begins with the *sk* blend as in *skirt:*

skip, stand?	*she, sky?*	*kill, skill?*
slip, skid?	*skin, kit?*	*skip, step?*

er ir ur		
hurry hurried	hury huryd	hurry hurried
nurse	nurs	nurse
person	persun	person
cover covered	cuver cuverd	cover covered
better	better	better
first	first	first

her – er
girl – ir
burn – ur

60   Lesson 11

Hurry to the Doctor!

us	said (sed)
then	helping
burns (burnz)	looked (lookt)

"Hurry! Hurry!" said Mrs. Miller.
"Hurry to the doctor!"

The Millers hurried to Dr. Chan's office.
A nurse was in the office.
Mr. Miller said to the nurse, "Help us!"

Mrs. Miller said, "Hurry!
Get the doctor for us.
Tell her to look at my little girl first."

The nurse hurried to get the doctor.
"Three persons are hurt," the nurse said.
"One person's leg is burned.
One person's hands are burned.
And one person's fingers are burned."

First, Dr. Chan looked at Fern.
The doctor looked at the burns on her leg first.
Then the doctor covered her burns.

Dr. Chan said to the nurse,
"First, cover the burns on Mrs. Miller's hands.
Then, cover the burns on Mr. Miller's fingers."
The nurse covered the burns quickly.

Mr. Miller said, "Thank you for helping us."

Fern's burns were better.
Mrs. Miller's hands were better.
Mr. Miller's fingers were better.

Lesson 11   61

PRACTICE 3: Verb Ending *-ed*

T: (Write *yelled* on the board.) In this lesson and the last lesson, you have read several words with the ending *-ed*. This is one of them. Please read it. [S: yelled.] (Cover *-ed*.) What is the word without the ending? [S: yell.] Remember, we call the word without the ending the *root word*. (Cover *yell*.) What is the ending? [S: *-ed*.] (Uncover *yell*.) Read the whole word again. [S: yelled.] How is the ending pronounced? [S: /d/.] How is it written? [S: ed.]

T: (Write *picked*.) This is another word with the ending *-ed*. But the *-ed* is pronounced in a different way. Read the word. [S: picked.] (Cover *-ed*.) What is the root word? [S: pick.] Good. (Cover *pick*.) What is the ending? [S: *-ed*.] How is the ending pronounced? [S: /t/.] How is it written? [S: ed.] The ending looks the same, but in *yelled* it is pronounced /d/ and in *picked* it is pronounced /t/.

T: I will say two words with the *-ed* ending. Which sound do you hear for the ending, /d/ or /t/:
burned, covered? [S: /d/.] *helped, fished?* [S: /t/.]
married, hurried? [S: /d/.] *lived, killed?* [S: /d/.]
thanked, jumped? [S: /t/.] *looked, stopped?* [S: /t/.]

T: (Write *visit*.) This is an old word to which you can add the ending *-ing*. What is the word? [S: visit.] Listen to the word with the *-ed* ending: *visited*. This time, the ending *-ed* is pronounced /ud/. (Add *-ed* to *visit* on the board.) Read the word with the ending. [S: visited.]

T: (Write *hunt*.) Read this word. [S: hunt.] What would the word be with the *-ed* ending? [S: hunted.]

T: You have learned three ways to pronounce the *-ed* ending. How is it pronounced in *covered*? [S: /d/.] In *picked*? [S: /t/.] In *visited*? [S: /ud/.]

PRACTICE 4: Subtracting *-ing*

T: This lesson also had some words with the *-ing* ending. I will say a word. Tell me what the root word is. Remember, the root word is the word without the ending.

T: What is the root word:
running? [S: run.] *getting?* [S: get.]
burning? [S: burn.] *looking?* [S: look.]
yelling? [S: yell.] *visiting?* [S: visit.]

60   Lesson 11

III. Writing

CHECK HOMEWORK: Page 57

Check this page with S. Have him correct any errors.

WRITING LESSON: Page 62

Study: Words ending in *er*. List these words on the board: *her, father, better, Miller, cover, finger*. Have S. read the words. Point out that each word ends with *er*. Help S. study each word except *finger* (a review word). Call attention to these points:

father — a for the sound /o/, *th* for the sound /th/.
better — double *t*.
Miller — capital *M*, double *l*.
cover — o for the sound /u/; *c* for the sound /k/ before *o*.

Have S. write *father* and *cover* by numbers 1 and 2 in the "Study" section of page 62.

Study: Other words with *er*. List these words on the board: *were, person, Fern*. Have S. read them and tell how the sound /er/ is written. Call attention to the silent *e* at the end of *were* and the *o* in *person*. Have S. write *were* and *person* by numbers 3 and 4 in the "Study" section.

Study: Words with *ur*. List these words on the board: *curtains, burn, burning, hurry, hurried, nurse, hurt*. Have S. read them and tell how the sound /er/ is written. Call attention to these points:

curtains — ai for the sound /u/; *c* for the sound /k/
   before *u*.
burning — the root word is *burn;* the ending is *-ing*.
hurry — double *r*; the letter *y* as a vowel.
hurried — the root word is *hurry*, but with the *y* changed
   to *i;* the ending is *-ed*.
nurse — silent *e* at the end.

Have S. write *curtains, hurried,* and *nurse* by numbers 5, 6, and 7 under "Study."

Study: Words with *ir*. Write these words: *girl, skirt, first*. Have S. read the words and tell how the sound /er/ is written. Call attention to the consonant blend *sk* in *skirt*. Be sure S. can say the letters in *first* in the right order. If he has trouble, refer to column 3 of the chart. Have him say each sound and the name of the letter or letters that stand for it.

Have S. write *girl* by number 8 under "Study."

Listen and write. Dictate these words for S. to write:

1. burn	5. better
2. hurry	6. fingers
3. hurt	7. skirt
4. her	8. first

Check your student's work. Have him correct any errors by erasing the whole word and writing it again.

HOMEWORK: Page 63

Go over the directions with S. Ask him to read both charts and stories in Lesson 11 again at home.

CHECKING PROGRESS

Word recognition. Check your student's progress in word recognition by having him read the flash cards for all chart words through Lesson 10. This will be a review of all short vowel sounds. Put in one pile the words that he was able to read easily, in another pile the words that he needed to sound out, and in a third pile any words he wasn't able to read. Keep these piles separate for further practice, or list the words he needs to study.

Vowel sounds. Have flash cards on hand for the vowels *a, e, i, o, u*. Say the following words, and have S. point to the vowel that stands for the short vowel sound he hears in each word. If he makes an error, jot down the vowel he should have said. When he finishes, note which vowel sound was hard for him to distinguish.

1. cat	6. hit	11. ten	16. cot
2. hot	7. red	12. bit	17. fun
3. nut	8. sad	13. doll	18. top
4. hat	9. but	14. lick	19. bell
5. net	10. Miss	15. glass	20. fuss

There are four words for each vowel sound. So, if S. misses any vowel more than once, it will indicate that he needs more practice on that vowel sound.

MEETING INDIVIDUAL NEEDS

Using flash cards, give further practice with any words that S. is not able to read easily. Help him blend the sounds and read the word.

If he needs extra practice with vowel sounds, see the suggestions in Lesson 10. If he frequently confuses the same two sounds—/o/ and /u/, for example—use only words with those vowel sounds in the practice exercises. It may also help S. if, when you are asking him to identify the vowel sound in a particular word, you say the word and then give a sentence using the word.

In *More Stories 2,* the stories for Lesson 10 may be read in class or suggested for reading at home.

Practices 11A–11E in *Focus on Phonics 2* may be used after Lesson 11. Practice 11B gives additional work on adding the ending *-ed* to words. The others are the remaining practices on the short vowel sound for *o*.

Study.

1. father   5. curtains
2. cover   6. hurried
3. were   7. nurse
4. person   8. girl

Listen and write.

1. burn   5. better
2. hurry   6. fingers
3. hurt   7. skirt
4. her   8. first

Fill in the letters.

fern   burning

skirt   nurse

father   girl

Fill in the words.

1. A match burned the **curtains**.
2. His fingers were **burned**.
3. Mrs. Miller said,
   "**Hurry** to the doctor."
4. Dr. Chan **covered** the burns.

LESSON 12

Book 2
Pages 64–69

OBJECTIVES

To help your student:

- recognize the sound /ar/ as in *arms* and the way it is written: *ar*.
- recognize the ending -*er* as in *farmer*.
- recognize the contraction *let's* and how it is formed.
- review the use of *k* for the sound /k/ after a consonant, as in *dark,* and the use of *ck* for the sound /k/ after a short vowel, as in *back*.
- review the use of *c* for the sound /k/ before the letter *a*, as in *car*.
- read the following new words in two charts and stories:

  Chart words: *arms, farm, farmer, Carmen, barn, garden, jar*

  Story words: *Carl, Arthur, hard, large, jelly, work, working*

  Chart words: *car, far, dark, market, parking, start, starting*

  Story words: *let's*.
- read two stories, using the new chart and story words.
- scan a page to find certain parts of the story.
- form new words by adding the endings -*er, -ing, -s,* and -*ed* to known reading words.
- review the endings -*s'* as in *farmers'* and *Arthurs'*.
- write the new chart and story words.

INTRODUCTION

T: In today's lesson, you will study one more sound. That will complete the sounds in this book.

I. Reading

CHART: Page 64

Title and key word. Have S. read the lesson title and tell what the letters are at the top left [*ar*].

T: (Point to picture of *arms.*) Look at this picture and the word next to it. The word is *arms*. Please read it. [S: arms.] *Arms* begins with the sound /ar/. Say /ar/. [S: /ar/.] Look at the letters under the word. What are the letters? [S: *ar*.] What sound do they stand for? [S: /ar/.] Read the word again. [S: arms.]

Lines 1–6 Teach the chart as in previous lessons. Call attention to the sound /ar/ in each word. Also point out the sound /er/ in *farmer*. In *Carmen,* point out that *c* is used for the sound /k/ because it is followed by *a*.

Review. Have S. read all of the words again, beginning with the key word *arms* and going down column 4.

STORY: Page 65 (The Arthurs' Farm)

Have S. read the title. Call attention to the -*s'* in *Arthurs'*. Explain that *Arthur* is a family name in this story and this ending with the apostrophe after the *s* means that the farm belongs to the *family,* not to just one person. (This is a review of -*s',* which was introduced in Lesson 2.)

Have S. study the new words silently and then read them aloud. Call attention to the sound /ar/ in *Carl, hard, Arthur, large*. Point out the /th/ sound in *Arthur*. Also point out the /er/ sound in *Arthur* and its regular spelling, *ur*. In *work* and *working,* point out that the /er/ sound is respelled because *or* is not always /er/.

Directed silent reading. Have S. read the whole story silently. Ask him to find out two things about the Arthurs and two things about their farm. When he finishes, have him tell what he found out. (Answers will vary.)

Scanning and oral reading. Have S. scan the story to find each part listed below. Tell him to look through the story quickly to find the part you describe. Remind him not to read everything, but to let his eyes run down the page until he finds the right part. Have him read each part aloud when he finds it.

1. The paragraph that tells about the barn.
2. The sentence that tells what kind of jelly they have.
3. The sentence that tells why Carmen's arms are hard.
4. The sentence that tells what Mr. and Mrs. Arthur are.
5. The paragraph that tells about their garden.
6. The sentence that tells what they will do with the jelly.

CHART: Page 66

Have S. tell what the letters at top left are, read the key word, and tell what sound the letters *ar* stand for.

Lines 1–6 Tell S. that the words in this chart are pronounced the way they are written. Have him study the chart and read the words to himself. When he has finished, have him read each word aloud. Call his attention to these points:

1. The /ar/ sound in each word.
2. Rhyming words *car* and *far*.
3. The use of *k* for the sound /k/ in *dark, market,* and *parking*. Point out that, in each of these words, /k/ follows a consonant.
4. The ending -*ing* in *parking* and *starting*.
5. The *st* blend in *start* and *starting*.

Review. Have S. read all of the words again, going down the last column of the chart.

STORY: Page 67 (At the Farmers' Market)

Have S. read the title and tell what the -*s'* ending means. Have him read the new word *let's*. Explain this word as in the next paragraph.

ar

arms
ar

	farm	farm	farm
	farmer	farmer	farmer
	Carmen	Carmen	Carmen
	barn	barn	barn
	garden	garden	garden
	jar	jar	jar

The Arthurs' Farm

Carl	jelly
Arthur	work (werk)
hard	working (werking)
large (larj)	

This is Carl Arthur.
This is Carmen Arthur.
Carl is a farmer.
Carmen is a farmer.
Mr. and Mrs. Arthur are farmers.

The Arthurs have a farm.
They have a large farm.
The Arthurs work hard.
They work hard on their large farm.

Carl's arms are hard.
His arms are hard from working on the farm.
Carmen's arms are hard.
Her arms are hard from working on the farm.

This is the Arthurs' barn.
The barn is on the farm.
The barn is very large.

This is the Arthurs' garden.
It is a large garden.
Carl and Carmen work hard in the garden.

This is a jar of jelly.
The Arthurs have many jars of jelly.
They have jars of apple jelly.
They will sell the jars of jelly.

ar

arms
ar

	car	car	car
	far	far	far
	dark	dark	dark
	market	market	market
	parking	parking	parking
	start starting	start starting	start starting

At the Farmers' Market

let's

This is the Arthurs' car.
Carl and Carmen are in their car.
They are going to the market.
The farmers' market is in the city.

The market is not far.
It is not far from the Arthurs' farm.
The Arthurs get to the market quickly in their car.

Many farmers are parking cars.
They are parking their cars at the market.
Carl is parking the car.
He is parking the car at the market.

The Arthurs sell apples and eggs at the market.
They sell hens at the market.
They sell jars of jelly at the market.

The Arthurs visit with friends at the market.

It is getting dark at the market.
The farmers will not sell after dark.
Carmen says, "It is getting dark.
Let's get in the car.
Let's start back to the farm."

Carl says, "Yes, it is getting dark.
Let's start back to the farm."

Carmen is starting the car.
The Arthurs are starting back to the farm.
It is not far to the farm.
It is not far from the market to the farm.

FRESH EGGS

Apple Jelly

T: The word *let's* has an apostrophe, but the apostrophe has a different meaning. *Let's* is a short form of two words: *let us*. (Write *let us* on the board.) When they are put together to make one word, a letter is left out. (Write *let's* under *let us*.) What letter is left out? [S: *u*.] An apostrophe is used in *let's* in place of the *u* that is left out. Read the word again. (Point to *let's* in student's book.) [S: let's.]

Directed silent reading. Ask S. to read the whole story to himself to find out three things about the market. When he finishes, have him tell what he found out.

Scanning. Have S. scan the page to find each part described below. When he has found the part, have him read it aloud.

1. The paragraph that tells what the Arthurs sell.
2. The paragraph that tells what the Arthurs do at the market besides selling things.
3. The sentence that tells who parks the Arthurs' car.
4. The sentences that tell what Carmen says when it gets dark.
5. The sentence that tells who starts the car when it is time to go home.

Oral reading. Have S. read both stories, on pages 65 and 67, aloud.

Reading between the lines. Discuss these questions with S. in relation to the two stories.

1. Do both of the Arthurs work on their farm? [Yes.]
2. Do both of them work in the garden? [Yes.]
3. Would you expect to find apple trees on their farm? Why? [Yes. They probably make the apple jelly that they sell from apples they grow.]
4. Who drives *to* the market, Carl or Carmen? How do you know? [Carl. He's the one who parks the car when they get to the market.]
5. Who drives home? [Carmen.]
6. Is the farmers' market open at night? How can you tell? [No. The story says that the farmers will not sell after dark.]
7. Is the Arthurs' farm a short way or a long way from the market? [A short way. The story says it's not far.]

Relating the story to everyday life. Ask S. if he has ever lived on a farm or if he has a garden. If so, let him tell about things he has grown. If there is a farmers' market in your area, talk about where it is, when it is open, and what you can buy there.

II. Skills Practice

T: Please close your book. We will have some exercises on adding some endings to words. And we will practice spelling the sound /k/ in words.

PRACTICE 1: Verb Endings *-s, -ing, -ed*

Write *work, start, park, farm* in a column. Have S. read the words. Tell him he can make new words by adding endings to these action words.

Have S. tell what each word would be with the ending *-s*. As he answers, write *works, starts, parks, farms* in column 2.

Have S. tell what each word would be with the ending *-ing*. As he answers, write *working, starting, parking, farming* in column 3.

Have S. tell what each word would be with the ending *-ed*. As he answers, write *worked, started, parked, farmed* in column 4.

Finally, have S. read all four forms of each word.

PRACTICE 2: Ending *-er*

T: We can also make new words by adding the ending *-er*.

Nouns with *-er*. Write *farm, hunt, work, start, burn* in a column. Have S. tell what each word would be with the ending *-er*. As he answers, write *farmer, hunter, worker, starter, burner* in column 2. Then have S. read both forms of each word.

T: (Point to column 2.) The *-er* ending makes these words mean *a person or thing that does something*. A farmer is a person that farms. A burner is a thing that burns.

Adjectives with *-er*. Write *dark, hard, quick, large* in a column. Have S. tell what each word would be with the ending *-er*. As he answers, write *darker, harder, quicker, larger* in column 2. (Explain that since *large* ends in *e*, we just add *-r*, not *-er*.) Then have S. read both forms of each word.

T: (Point to column 2.) The *-er* ending in these words means *more*. For example, *darker* means *more dark*.

PRACTICE 3: Endings *-'s* and *-s'*

T: (Write this sentence: *Carl's arms are hard*. Have S. read it.) Whose arms are hard? [S: Carl's.] Do the arms belong to one person or more than one person? [S: One.] Where does the apostrophe come, before or after the *s*? [S: Before the *s*.]

T: (Write this sentence: *This is the Arthurs' car*. Have S. read it.) Whose car is it? [S: The Arthurs'.] Does the car belong to one person or more than one person? [S: More than one person.] Where does the apostrophe come? [S: After the *s*.]

Make two columns with the headings *-'s* and *-s'*. Read the sentences below. Have S. listen for the word with the *-'s* or *-s'* ending, tell what the word is, and which ending it has. Write the word in the correct column.

1. The *Arthurs'* farm is large.
2. Carmen is *Carl's* wife.
3. The *farmers'* market is in the city.
4. Fern is the *Millers'* daughter.
5. *Fern's* skirt was burning.

Study.

1. large   3. Arthur
2. garden   4. work

Listen and write.

1. farm   5. hard
2. barn   6. car
3. arms   7. far
4. farmer   8. dark

Listen and write.

1. Carl is parking the car.
2. The market is not far.
3. Carmen and Carl are farmers.

Fill in the letters.

barn   person
farmer parking
arms   market

Fill in the words.

1. The Arthurs have a farm.
2. They work hard.
3. The barn is large.
4. This is a jar of jelly.
5. Let's get in the car.

PRACTICE 4: Spellings of the Sound /k/

At the end of a word: *k* or *ck*. On the board, write the words *dark, park, work, thank*. Have S. read the words.

T: What sound do these words end with? [S: /k/.] What comes before the /k/ sound, a vowel or a consonant? [S: A consonant.] Remember the rule: when the sound /k/ comes after a consonant, it is usually written with *k*.

Write *back, duck, sick, rock* on the board, and have S. read these words.

T: What letters are used for the sound /k/ in these words? [S: *ck*.] What kind of sound does /k/ come after? [S: A short vowel sound.] Remember this rule: when the sound /k/ comes after a short vowel sound, it is usually written with *ck*.

Say each of the following words, and have S. tell you whether it ends with *k* or *ck:*

| brick | think | mark | pick | bank | park |
| clock | quick | milk | ask | pack | truck |

At the beginning of a word: *c* or *k*. On the board, write the words *car, come, cut, clock*. Have S. read them.

T: What sound do these words begin with? [S: /k/.]
    What letter is used for the sound /k/?   [S: *c*.]
    What letter comes after *c* in *car*?   [S: *a*.]
    What letter comes after *c* in *come*?   [S: *o*.]
    What letter comes after *c* in *cut*?   [S: *u*.]
    What letter comes after *c* in *clock*?   [S: *l*.]
    Is *l* a vowel or a consonant?   [S: A consonant.]

T: Remember this rule: when the sound /k/ comes before *a, o, u,* or a consonant, it is usually written with *c*.

Write *Kim* and *Ken*. Have S. read the words. Help him sound out the name *Ken* if he needs help.

T: What sound do these words begin with? [S: /k/.]
    What letter is used for the sound /k/?   [S: *k*.]
    What letter comes after *k* in *Kim*?   [S: *i*.]
    What letter comes after *k* in *Ken*?   [S: *e*.]

T: Remember this rule: when the sound /k/ comes before *e* or *i*, it is usually written with *k*.

Say each of the following words, and have S. tell you whether it begins with *c* or *k*:

| can | Kitty | car | cover | kitchen | copy |
| kill | Carl | kick | curtains | Carmen | kept |

III. Writing

CHECK HOMEWORK: Page 63

Check this page with S. Have him correct any errors.

WRITING LESSON: Page 68

Study. Help S. study and write these words: (1) *large,* (2) *garden,* (3) *Arthur,* (4) *work.* Call his attention to the /ar/ sound in the first three words. In *large,* point out that *g* is used for the /j/ sound and that it is followed by a silent *e.* In *Arthur,* have S. tell the names of the letters that stand for the /er/ sound. In *work,* point out that the letters *or* are used for the sound /er/. Ask S. how he can tell that the sound /k/ should be written with *k*. [It comes after a consonant.]

Listen and write. Dictate these words for S. to write: (1) *farm,* (2) *barn,* (3) *arms,* (4) *farmer,* (5) *hard,* (6) *car,* (7) *far,* (8) *dark.* Check his work and have him correct any errors by rewriting the whole word.

Then have S. cover the top half of the page. Dictate these sentences for him to write:

1. Carl is parking the car.
2. The market is not far.
3. Carmen and Carl are farmers.

Check his work for spelling and punctuation. Have S. correct any errors.

HOMEWORK: Page 69

Go over the directions with S. Ask him to study all the charts in book 2 as the next lesson will be a review of the vowel sounds, blends, and new consonant sounds that he has had in this book.

CHECKING PROGRESS

You may use the following suggestions to check your student's progress in some of the reading comprehension skills developed in this book.

Sequence of events. Write these sentences on flash cards or strips of paper:

The Arthurs are going to the market.
Carl is parking the car.
The Arthurs sell apples and eggs at the market.
It is getting dark at the market.
Carmen is starting the car.
The Arthurs are starting back to the farm.

Mix up the sentences. Have S. arrange them in the order in which they happened in the story. (The correct order is given above.) If S. has a sentence out of order, have him check back with the story.

Summarizing the main ideas. Have S. read the one-page story "The Glass Factory Burns" in *More Stories 2.* (It is one of the three stories for Lesson 11.) Ask him to summarize it in his own words.

Interpreting the emotions of the characters. Have S. reread the story "Hunting with Ed and Cal" in *More Stories 2.* (This is one of the stories for Lesson 8.) Then ask these questions:

1. How does Ed feel after waiting for Cal? [Worried.]
2. What does Ed think might have happened to Cal? [He is afraid that Cal has been hurt or killed.] Why does Ed think that might have happened? [There is another hunter there shooting his gun.]
3. What shows that Ed gets more concerned? [He goes to look for Cal.]
4. How does Ed feel after he finds Cal? [Thankful that Cal isn't dead.]
5. (In this question, use the "emotion words" that S. has used in his answers.) Are the words *worried, afraid,* and *thankful* used in the story? [No.] Then how can we tell how Ed feels? [From what he thinks and does in the story.]

Note which of these comprehension skills S. finds difficult, and plan similar exercises to give him more help.

MEETING INDIVIDUAL NEEDS

If you think S. needs more practice with the /er/ sound and its spellings, these exercises may be helpful:

1. Put the following words on flash cards. Mix them up. Have S. read the words and then sort the cards into three piles according to the way the sound /er/ is written: *er, ir, ur.*

her	*father*	*girl*	*hurt*	*hurried*
were	*better*	*bird*	*burn*	*curtains*
Fern	*person*	*skirt*	*nurse*	
cover	*Miller*	*first*	*hurry*	

2. Make a set of flash cards for each list below. Lay out the *er* words in a row. Mix up the names. Have S. match each name to the word that describes that person.

mother	*Mrs. Hill*
father	*Mr. Hill*
sister	*Jill*
brother	*Ed*

3. Review the other words ending in *er* from Lessons 1–10 and from book 1. Write the words listed below on the board. Have S. read each word and underline the letters that stand for the sound /er/.

after	*letter*	*river*	*Fisher*
dinner	*number*	*under*	*Oliver*
finger	*quarter*	*zipper*	*Robert*

In *More Stories 2,* the stories for Lesson 11 may be read in class or suggested for reading at home.

In *Focus on Phonics 2,* Practice 12 is about the ending *-es,* as in *match, matches.* You may use this practice after Lesson 12. Or, you may think it would be better for your student if you saved this practice until the *-es* ending is introduced in Lesson 14.

OBJECTIVES

To help your student:

- review the short vowel sounds represented by the letters *a, e, i, o, u* and the vowel sound for *y* as in *lily,* and identify these sounds in words.
- review the sound /er/ represented by *er, ir, ur* and the sound /ar/ represented by *ar.*
- review the consonant sound /ng/ represented by *ng,* the sound /wh/ represented by *wh,* and the voiced /th/ sound represented by *th,* as in *that.*
- recognize the number of consonant sounds that come before a vowel sound in a word.
- review the beginning consonant blends *br, dr, fr, gr, pr, tr, bl, cl, gl, sk, sm, st, tw* and the ending consonant blends *nd, nt, nk, nch.*
- read familiar material fluently.
- scan to find a certain paragraph in a story.
- summarize a story in his own words.
- review sequence of events.
- recognize the following punctuation marks and how they are used: question mark, exclamation point, quotation marks.
- write the correct letter or letters for each sound of a word that is spelled the way it sounds.
- write sentences from dictation, using correct spelling and punctuation.

INTRODUCTION

T: Today's lesson is a review lesson. *Review* means that you will look over some of the things that you have already studied. This review lesson will help you remember the important things that you have covered in this book. First, we will review some of the stories.

I. Reading

STORY REVIEW

Page 7: A Ring for Kim. Have S. read the title and tell how many paragraphs are in this story [seven]. Have him find the paragraph that tells what gift Jill gives to Kim [par. 5]. Have him read this paragraph aloud.

Page 17: In the City. Have S. read the title. Ask him who the people in the story are [Kitty King, Jimmy Fisher]. Ask what title is used for Kitty King [Ms.]. Have S. find the words in which *y* is used as a vowel and read them aloud [*city, windy, Kitty, Jimmy, pretty*].

Have S. find the paragraph that tells what Kitty is giving to Jimmy [par. 6] and read it aloud.

Page 27: Uncle Bud's Truck Gets Stuck. Have S. read the title. Ask him who the people in the story are [Mrs. Hill, Ed Hill, Bud Buck—or Mr. Buck, or Uncle Bud.] Ask what relation Bud Buck is to Ed [his uncle] and what relation Bud is to Mrs. Hill [her brother].

Write quotation marks on the board. Ask S. what they are called and why they are used [to show what someone says]. Have S. find the paragraph that tells what Ed's mother says to Ed [par. 5], point to the quotation marks, and read just the part that she says.

Page 31: Eggs to Sell. Have S. read the title. Ask him to find the first question that Fred asks and read it aloud. ["Are the eggs fresh?"] Then ask him to read Ellen's answer. ["Yes, the eggs are very fresh."]

Ask S. to find the second question that Fred asks and read it aloud. ["Do you sell hens?"] Ask him what kind of mark is used at the end of a question [question mark]. Then have him read Ellen's answer. [S. reads what Ellen says in the last paragraph.]

Page 43: Jack and Ann Will Marry. Have S. read the title and tell how many paragraphs are in the story [six]. Ask him to find the paragraph that tells how the Smith family feels [par. 6] and read it aloud.

Page 53: At the Doctor's Office. Have S. read the title. Ask him to read the story quickly to himself and then tell it briefly in his own words.

Page 59: Fern Gets Burned. Have S. read the title and the new story words at the top of the page.

Write an exclamation point. Ask S. what it is called and what it means [excitement, or similar answer]. Ask him to find the first sentence with an exclamation point and read it aloud. [Fern yelled, "Help! I am burning !"] Ask him to find another sentence with an exclamation point and read it aloud. ["Fern's skirt is burning! Get a rug!"]

Page 67: At the Farmers' Market. Have S. read the title. Ask him to read the story to himself and be ready to tell the main events in the order they happened.

When S. is ready, have him tell the events in order. List them on the board as he tells them. The list may be as follows:

1. Carl and Carmen go to the farmers' market in the car.
2. Carl parks the car.
3. The Arthurs sell apples, eggs, hens, and jelly at the market.
4. The Arthurs visit with their friends.
5. When it is dark, the Arthurs get in the car.
6. Carmen starts the car.
7. They start back to the farm.

   Note: S. may tell the story in the past tense. But, in listing the events, use the verb forms he can read, as in the list above.

Write *farmers' market* and *Arthurs' farm* on the board. Have S. read the words aloud. Ask him if the *-s'* ending means belonging to one person or to more than one.

Oral reading. Let S. choose a story that he likes and have him read it aloud. Encourage him to read it with expression. Note his skill in reading fluently and in observing punctuation marks.

II. Skills Practice

T: Please close your book. We will review the sounds and consonant blends you have studied in this book.

PRACTICE 1: Short Vowel Sounds

Ask S. to name the vowels [*a, e, i, o, u, y*]. List them in a column as he says them. Ask him to say the key word that he has had for each vowel and to give the sound for the vowel in that word. If he doesn't remember a key word, write it and have him read the word. The key words are: *apple, egg, in, olive, up, lily.*

T: I will say three words. Listen for the vowel sound that is the same in all three words. Tell me the vowel sound and the key word for that sound.

T: *sit, hit, this*   [S: /i/, *in.*]
  grass, at, bag   [S: /a/, *apple.*]
  let, well, fresh,   [S: /e/, *egg.*]
  cup, gun, hunt   [S: /u/, *up.*]
  doll, rock, top   [S: /o/, *olive.*]
  city, funny, jelly   [S: /y/, *lily.*]

If S. doesn't give the vowel sound /y/ as the last answer, write the three words on the board and ask which vowel is the same in all three words.

PRACTICE 2: Sounds /er/ and /ar/

T: (Write *er, ir, ur* on the board.) As I point to the letters, tell me their names and the sound they stand for. [S: *er,* /er/; *ir,* /er/; *ur,* /er/.]

T: Which word has the sound /er/ in it:
  her, car?   *start, skirt?*   *bird, barn?*
  farm, burn?   *garden, girl?*   *Fern, Fred?*

T: (Write *ar* on the board.) Tell me the names of these letters and the sound they stand for. [S: *ar,* /ar/.]

T: Which word has the sound /ar/ in it:
  dark, dirt?   *hard, heard?*   *Carl, curl?*
  burn, barn?   *grass, garden?*   *farm, from?*

PRACTICE 3: Consonant Sounds /wh/, /th/, /ng/

T: (Write *whistle.*) Read this word. [S: whistle.]
  What sound does *whistle* begin with? [S: /wh/.]
  What letters stand for the sound /wh/? [S: *wh.*]

T: Which word begins with the sound /wh/ as in *whistle*:
  hen, when?   *which, hit?*   *will, what?*
  whip, hip?   *there, where?*   *which, wish?*

Note: S. Omit the words in the last column above if neither you nor S. pronounces *wh* differently from *w.*

T: (Write *that.*) Read this word. [S: that.]
  What sound does *that* begin with? [S: /th/.]
  What letters stand for the sound /th/? [S: *th.*]
  This is the *th* sound with more voice.
  We call it the voiced *th.*

T: Which word begins with the sound /th/ as in *that:*
  them, him?   *where, there?*   *Dan, than?*
  van, than?   *though, zoo?*   *they, day?*

T: (Write *ring.*) Read this word. [S: ring.]
  What consonant sound does *ring* end with [S: /ng/.]
  What letters stand for the sound /ng/? [S: *ng.*]

T: What word ends with the sound /ng/ as in *ring:*
  sun, sing?   *brick, bring?*   *rang, ran?*
  wing, wig?   *thing, thick?*   *hand, hang?*

PRACTICE 4: Beginning Consonant Blends

T: Listen to this word, and tell me how many consonant sounds you hear before the vowel sound: *brick.* [S: Two.] What are the sounds? [S: /br/.] What letters stand for the sounds? [S: *br.*] (Write brick, and underline *br.*) What do we call this blend? [S: *br.*]

Consonant blends *br, dr, fr, gr, pr, tr.* Write these blends on the board, and have S. give their names.

T: Which blend do these words begin with:
  Fred, fresh?   *drop, dress?*   *grass, green?*
  pretty, prom?   *truck, trip?*   *bring, bread?*

T: What letter is in each of these blends? [S: *r.*] How many sounds does each of these blends stand for? [S: Two.]

Consonant blends *bl, cl, gl.* Write these blends on the board, and have S. give their names.

T: Which blend do these words begin with:
  black, blank?   *glass, glad?*   *clock, class?*

T: What letter is in each of these blends? [S: *l.*] How many sounds does each of these blends stand for? [S: Two.]

Consonant blends *sk, sm, st, tw.* Write these blends on the board, and have S. give their names.

T: Which blend do these words begin with:
  skirt, skill?   *stuck, still?*   *twelve, twenty?*
  Smith, smile?   *sky, skate?*   *stop, start?*

T: How many sounds does each of these blends stand for? [S: Two.] (Cover the *tw* blend and point to others.) What letter is in these three blends? [S: *s.*]

PRACTICE 5: Ending Consonant Blends *nd, nt, nk, nch*

Write *send, hunt, think, lunch* on the board. Have S. read each word and tell what consonant blend it ends with. As he answers, underline *nd, nt, nk, nch.*

T: Which blend do these words end with:
  tent, cent?   *hand, wind?*   *went, plant?*
  pink, thank?   *inch, ranch?*   *send, friend?*

Lesson 13

Listen and write.

1. bed
2. run
3. it
4. bell
5. stand
6. windy
7. rock
8. first
9. arm
10. burn
11. father
12. car
13. grass
14. drop
15. ring
16. singing
17. lunch
18. hat
19. sang
20. trash

Listen and write.

1. This is a big city.
2. The sun is up.
3. Ellen Bell sells eggs.
4. Is Fred very sick?
5. Fern's father ran to help her.
6. The truck is stuck.
7. The farmer parks his car.
8. Kim is Ed's sister.
9. The girl is singing.
10. Are the eggs in a box?

Homework

copy, add, what (whut)

Fill in the letters.

 m e n

 c i t y

 g u n

 b a c k

 d o ll

 fath e r

 sk i r t

 n u r se

Copy the word. Add -er. What is the word?

1. farm **farmer**   3. work
2. quick   4. hunt

Homework

Fill in the letters.

 Miss

 whistle

 ring

 kit c hen

path

s h op

Fill in the words.

1. Kim is Ed's little __sister__.
2. Mrs. Hill is Ed's __mother__.
3. Mr. Hill is Ed's __father__.
4. Ed is Mr. Hill's __son__.
5. Ed is Kim's __brother__.

III. Writing

CHECK HOMEWORK: Page 69

Check this page with S. Have him correct any errors.

WRITING LESSON: Page 70

Have S. read the lesson title, the title *Writing Lesson,* and the directions *Listen and write.* Explain that you will dictate 20 words for him to write. Tell him that the words are written the way they sound. The words are:

1. bed	6. windy	11. father	16. singing
2. run	7. rock	12. car	17. lunch
3. it	8. first	13. grass	18. hat
4. bell	9. arm	14. drop	19. sang
5. stand	10. burn	15. ring	20. trash

(The last three words are new, but S. should be able to write them from listening to the sounds.) Check his work, and have him correct any errors by erasing the whole word and writing it again.

WRITING LESSON: Page 71

Dictate the following sentences for S. to write. Remind him to use capitals and punctuation.

1. This is a big city.
2. The sun is up.
3. Ellen Bell sells eggs.
4. Is Fred very sick?
5. Fern's father ran to help her.
6. The truck is stuck.
7. The farmer parks his car.
8. Kim is Ed's sister.
9. The girl is singing.
10. Are the eggs in a box?

Check what S. has written. Help him correct any errors.

HOMEWORK: Pages 72–73

Go over the directions with S. Call his attention to the new words: *copy, add, what.*

Suggest that he study any words missed in the Writing Lesson. Encourage him to read some of the stories again at home.

CHECKING PROGRESS

This review lesson will help you check your student's progress. Look over the list of skills given in the Introduction to book 2 in this manual. Put a check by those skills in which your student's progress seems satisfactory. Note those in which he needs more practice. If he is weak in several skills, you may want to plan a supplementary lesson before he goes on to Lesson 14.

MEETING INDIVIDUAL NEEDS

If S. needs more review, use any of the suggestions in this manual that would be helpful. If he needs more practice with /er/ and /ar/ words, use any of the following exercises that suit his needs.

1. If S. has trouble seeing the difference between words with *ar* and those with short *a,* make flash cards for pairs of similar words, such as these:

am, arm	*pack, park*
had, hard	*Cal, Carl*

Work with one pair of cards at a time. Ask S. which word has the sound /ar/, and have him underline the letters that stand for /ar/. Have him read both words. Then say a sentence using one of the words, and repeat the word. (For example, say: "My *arm* is tired. *Arm.*") Have S. pick the correct card. Give two or three sentences for each pair of words.

2. If S. has trouble seeing the difference between words with spellings for /er/ and those with spellings for /e/, /i/, /u/, do a similar exercise with these word pairs:

hen, her	*hunt, hurt*	*head, heard*
gift, girl	*fish, first*	

It may help to cross lightly through the *a* in *head* and *heard* to remind S. that it is silent in these words.

3. If S. has trouble distinguishing words with *ar* from those with various spellings for /er/, do a similar exercise with these word pairs:

barn, burn	*start, skirt*
farm, fern	*hard, heard*

Ask S. which word has the sound /ar/ and what letters stand for the sound. As he answers, underline *ar.* Ask him which word has the sound /er/ and what letters stand for that sound. Underline the letters, using a different color. (Again, it may help if you lightly cross out the silent *a* in *heard.*)

4. If S. has trouble distinguishing /er/ and /ar/ words from those that have beginning blends with *r,* make flash cards for these word pairs:

Fred, Fern	*bring, bird*	*grass, garden*
Fran, Fern	*brick, bird*	*pretty, person*
from, farm	*fresh, first*	*friend, farmer*

Work with one pair at a time. Ask S. which word begins with a consonant blend. When he answers, circle the blend. Then ask him which word has the sound /ar/—or /er/—in it. Underline the letters for that sound. Have S. read both words. Say a sentence using one of the words, and have him pick the correct card, as in number 1 above. Give two or three sentences for each pair.

In *More Stories 2,* the stories for Lesson 12 may be read in class or suggested for reading at home. If you are planning a supplementary lesson, you may use these or the stories for Lesson 13.

In *Focus on Phonics 2,* Practices 13A–13B may be used after Lesson 13. They cover the ending *-er.* 13A is about the adjective ending *-er,* as in *dark, darker.* 13B is about the noun ending *-er,* as in *farm, farmer.*

In this lesson, S. begins reading the correlated reader *City Living*. Be sure that it is available at this time. No pages from *City Living* are reproduced here.

OBJECTIVES

To help your student:

- use a table of contents.
- read the first two stories in *City Living* independently, understanding the main ideas.
- increase speed of silent reading.
- scan a story to locate specific details.
- review words learned in book 2 by recognizing them in a new book.
- read the following new words in *City Living*:
  Cover: *living*
  Story 1:   *coming, other, watching, dad, kiss, watches, laughing, kisses, kissing*
  Story 2:   *dress, dresses, marked, twenty, hats, six, asks, but, fit, slim, pink, matches.*
- read the following new words in the skill book:
  Page 74: *who, color*
  Page 75: *circle, or.*
- check comprehension by giving oral answers to written questions and by reading and answering Yes/No questions.
- recognize the consonant blend *sl* as in *slim.*
- review the beginning consonant blends *bl, gl, br, dr, pr, sk, sm, tw.*
- recognize the ending consonant blend *sk* as in *ask.*
- understand that the ending *-es* is added instead of *-s* when the root word ends in *s, sh, ch,* or *x.*
- recognize root words in words with the *-ed* ending.

INTRODUCTION

T: Today you will begin a new book. It is a series of stories that you can read by yourself. Today you will read two of the stories. After you finish a story, you will read and answer some questions about the story to see if you understood what you read. The questions are in your skill book.

I. Reading in *City Living*

Give S. his copy of *City Living*. Point out the title on the cover, and have S. read it. Point out the series title *Laubach Way to Reading*, read it for S., and have him read it after you.

Have S. read the title *City Living* again on the title page. Then ask him to turn the page and look at page 3.

T: This is called the *contents page*. It lists the titles of all the stories in the book. It also tells what page each story begins on. Read the title of the page. [S: Contents.]

T: Today you will read the first two stories. What is the title of story number 1? [S: Jack Black Comes to the City.] What page does it begin on? [S: Page 5.]

T: What is the title of story number 2? [S: At the Dress Shop.] What page does it begin on? [S: Page 9.] Please turn to the first story on page 5.

STORY 1: Jack Black Comes to the City

Silent reading (pages 5–8 in *City Living*). Have S. read aloud the story title and the new words on pages 5, 6, and 8. On page 8, call attention to the *-es* ending in *kisses* and *watches*. Be sure S. understands that the story ends on page 8.

T: In the skill book, you read two stories about Jack Black. This first story tells more about him and Ann. Please read the whole story to yourself. Find out why Jack comes to the city and what he brings with him. Also, find out what Jack and Ann will do.

T: Read the story quickly and also carefully. Let me know when you have finished.

Time your student's reading. Try to do this without his noticing. He should be able to finish in 10 to 15 minutes. Make a note of the time, but don't comment on it. If it seems necessary, exercises can be planned later to help him increase speed. The most important thing now is for him to read independently and to understand what he reads.

When S. has finished, have him answer the questions that you asked to direct his reading.

T: Why did Jack come to the city? [S: To live and work. To visit the Smiths.] What did he bring with him? [S: A basket of apples for the Smiths and a ring for Ann.] What will Ann and Jack do? [S: Marry.]

Study helps (page 74 in book 2). Have S. read the titles *Lesson 14* and *Study Helps for City Living.*

T: On this page, there are some questions about the first two stories in *City Living*. Look at the new words under the title. The first word is a question word. You haven't had all the sounds in this word, so I'll tell you what it is. The word is *who*. Please read it. [S: who.] You can sound out the next word. What is it? [S: color.]

Have S. read the heading *Jack Black Comes to the City* over the first set of questions. Have him read each question silently and then aloud. Then ask him to give the answer. If he doesn't remember it, let him look back at the story. Encourage him to scan the story to find the answer. Then have him read aloud the part that answers the question.

STORY 2: At the Dress Shop

Silent reading (pages 9–12 in *City Living*). Have S. read the story title aloud. Have him read the new words on each page silently and then aloud. Help him sound out the words if he needs help.

Ask S. to read the whole story to himself to find out who is shopping at the dress shop and what she buys. Also, ask him to find out who works at the dress shop. Be sure S. understands that the story ends on page 12.

Again, time your student's reading. He will probably finish in about 10 minutes. When he finishes, have him answer the questions you asked to direct his reading. If he doesn't remember or answers incorrectly, have him scan the story to find the correct answer.

Study helps (page 74 in book 2). Have S. read the heading *At the Dress Shop* over the second set of questions. Help him read the word *address* in question 1 (he may not remember this review word from book 1).

Have S. read each question aloud and answer it. Let him scan the story for the answer if he needs to. If he can't find the answer, tell him the page and paragraph, and have him read that part aloud.

Finally, ask S. if he thinks Ann is a good salesperson. Have him tell some things she did in the story that helped him form his opinion.

CHECKUP: Page 75 in book 2

Have S. read the title. Explain that this Checkup is about the first two stories in *City Living*. Have S. read the first new word, *circle*. Tell him the other new word, *or*, and have him read it after you.

Have S. read the direction *Circle yes or no*. Then have him read the sample question and tell which answer is circled. Have him read the directions *Fill in the words* at the bottom of the page.

Have S. do this Checkup in class. Go over it with him when he has finished. Help him find the correct answers in the stories if he missed any.

II. Skills Practice

T: Please close your book. We will have some exercises on consonant blends and on adding endings to words.

PRACTICE 1: Beginning Consonant Blend *sl*

T: (Write *slim*.) Read this word. [S: slim.] What consonant sounds do you hear before the vowel sound? [S: /sl/.] What letters stand for the sounds? [S: *sl*.] (Underline *sl*.) We call this the *sl* blend.

T: Which word begins with the *sl* blend as in *slim:*

slip, sip?	led, sled?	stop, slap?
so, slow?	leap, sleep?	slant, plant?

PRACTICE 2: Review of *bl, gl, br, dr, pr, sk, sm, tw*

Write these words: *black, glass, bring, dress, pretty, skirt, Smith, twenty*. Have S. read each word and tell what blend it begins with. Underline each blend.

T: Which blend do these words begin with:

drop, drag?	glad, glove?	twelve, twist?
skin, skip?	price, prop?	smell, smart?
twin, twig?	blue, block?	brick, brother?

PRACTICE 3: Ending Consonant Blend *sk*

T: (Write *ask* on the board.) Read the word. [S: ask.] *Ask* ends with the consonant blend *sk*. (Underline *sk*.)

T: Which word ends with the blend *sk* as in *ask:*

desk, deck?	mass, mask?	desk, west?
tack, task?	brisk, brass?	risk, wrist?

PRACTICE 4: Ending *-es*

Words that end in s. Write *dresses* on the board, and have S. read it. Cover the *-es* ending, and ask what the root word is [*dress*]. Cover *dress*, and ask what the ending is [*-es*].

T: You have added the ending *-s* to some words. But if we added *-s* by itself to *dress*, the word would be hard to pronounce. So we add *-es*. If a word ends with the letter *s*, we add *-es* instead of *-s* to make a new word.

Write *kiss, glass*. Have S. read each word, tell what letter it ends with, whether we add *-s* or *-es*, and what the word is with the ending *-es* added. As he answers, write *kisses, glasses*.

Words that end in ch. Write *matches, watches*. Have S. read each word, tell what the ending is, and what the root word is. As he answers, write *match, watch*.

T: What sound do these root words end with? [S: /ch/.] What letters stand for the sound /ch/? [S: *ch*.] If a word ends in *ch*, we add *-es* instead of *-s*.

Words that end in sh. Write *dishes*. Have S. read the word, tell what the ending is, and what the root word is. As he answers, write *dish*.

T: What sound does *dish* end with? [S: /sh/.] What letters stand for the sound /sh/? [S: *sh*.] If a word ends in *sh*, we add *-es* instead of *-s*.

Write *fish*. Have S. read the word, tell whether we add *-s* or *-es*, and what the word is with the ending *-es* added. As he answers, write *fishes*.

Words that end in x. Follow the same procedure with the word *boxes* as you did for *dishes*. Point out that if a word ends with *x*, we add *-es* instead of *-s*. Use *fix* as another example.

PRACTICE 5: Verb Ending *-ed*

Write these words on the board in a column: *marked, watched, kissed, looked, laughed, visited, covered*.

Have S. read each word, tell what the root word is, what the ending is, and how the *-ed* ending is pronounced.

Study Helps for *City Living*

who   color (culer)

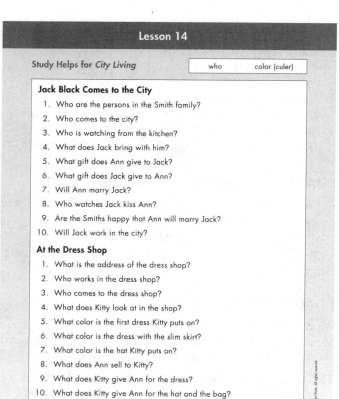

Jack Black Comes to the City

1. Who are the persons in the Smith family?
2. Who comes to the city?
3. Who is watching from the kitchen?
4. What does Jack bring with him?
5. What gift does Ann give to Jack?
6. What gift does Jack give to Ann?
7. Will Ann marry Jack?
8. Who watches Jack kiss Ann?
9. Are the Smiths happy that Ann will marry Jack?
10. Will Jack work in the city?

At the Dress Shop

1. What is the address of the dress shop?
2. Who works in the dress shop?
3. Who comes to the dress shop?
4. What does Kitty look at in the shop?
5. What color is the first dress Kitty puts on?
6. What color is the dress with the slim skirt?
7. What color is the hat Kitty puts on?
8. What does Ann sell to Kitty?
9. What does Kitty give Ann for the dress?
10. What does Kitty give Ann for the hat and the bag?

---

circle (sircul), or

Circle yes or no.

Is Jack coming to the city? (Yes) No

1. Will Jack visit the Smith family? (Yes) No
2. Is Jack bringing fresh eggs? Yes (No)
3. Is Sam Jack's brother? Yes (No)
4. Does Ann give Jack a gift? (Yes) No
5. Does Jack give Ann a ring? (Yes) No
6. Will Ann marry Jack? (Yes) No
7. Does Ann work in a pet shop? Yes (No)
8. Does Ann help Kitty? (Yes) No
9. Does the red dress fit Kitty? Yes (No)
10. Does Kitty get a black dress? (Yes) No
11. Is the black dress seventy dollars? Yes (No)
12. Does Kitty get a hat and a bag? (Yes) No

Fill in the words.

1. Jack will **work** at the factory.

2. Jack will marry **Ann**.

3. Ann works in a **dress** shop.

Study.

1. watch   3. marked
2. other   4. twenty

Listen and write.

1. dad   5. asks
2. kiss   6. fit
3. dress   7. slim
4. hat   8. pink

Listen and write.

1. The dress is marked twenty dollars.

2. The pink bag matches the hat.

Copy the word. Add -s. What is the word?

1. hat **hats**   3. send
2. bag   4. pick

Copy the word. Add -es. What is the word?

1. kiss **kisses**   4. fix
2. dress   5. dish
3. watch

Copy the word. Add -ed. What is the word?

1. look **looked**   4. visit
2. mark   5. hand
3. watch

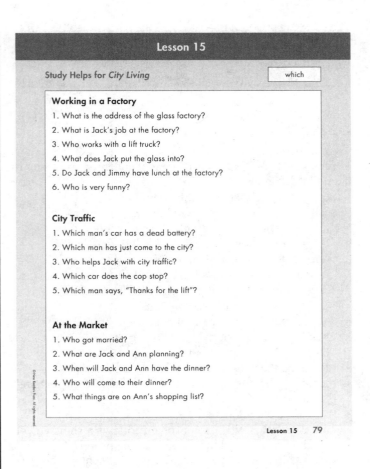

III. Writing

CHECK HOMEWORK: Pages 72–73

Check these pages with S. Have him correct any errors.

WRITING LESSON: Page 76

Study. Help S. study and write these words: (1) *watch*, (2) *other*, (3) *marked*, (4) *twenty*.

Listen and write. Dictate these words for S. to write: (1) *dad*, (2) *kiss*, (3) *dress*, (4) *hat*, (5) *asks*, (6) *fit*, (7) *slim*, (8) *pink*. Check his work, and have him correct any errors. Then have S. cover all but the last two lines, and dictate the sentences below for him to write. Check his work, and have him correct any errors.

1. The dress is marked twenty dollars.
2. The pink bag matches the hat.

WRITING LESSON: Page 77

This part of the Writing Lesson is about word endings. Have S. read the first directions. In number 1, which is done for him, have him read the root word and the word with the ending. Let him complete this part by himself. Check his work, and have him correct any errors.

Have S. read the directions for the other two parts. Then let him do them by himself. Check his work, and have him make any needed corrections.

HOMEWORK: Page 78

Have S. read the directions. Ask him to reread the first two stories in *City Living* at home and to read the third story, "Working in a Factory." Go over the new words in this story with him. Point out the Study Helps for this story in Lesson 15. Suggest that he read the questions and find the answers to be ready for your next class.

CHECKING PROGRESS

Note your student's ability in these skills when he is reading *City Living:*

1. Recognizes most of the words.
2. Understands main ideas.
3. Locates specific detail by scanning a page.
4. Observes punctuation marks.
5. Reads smoothly, in phrases, when reading aloud.

MEETING INDIVIDUAL NEEDS

If S. needs more practice in answering Yes/No questions, you can prepare a few written questions about one of the stories in *More Stories 2.* (Be sure to use words he can read.) The stories for Lesson 13 may be read in class or suggested for reading at home, if this will not interfere with the student's reading of *City Living*.

In *Focus on Phonics 2*, you may use Practice 12 on *-es* if you have not already done so.

OBJECTIVES

To help your student:

- read stories 3–5 in *City Living* independently, understanding the main ideas.
- scan a story to locate specific details.
- read the following new words in *City Living*:
  Story 3: *center, lot, just, started, boxes, lift, let, drop, into, any, carry, having, fun*
  Story 4: *traffic, dead, battery, fast, turn, pass, passes, must, when, cop, stopping, thinking*
  Story 5: *married, planning, past, list, things, bread, butter, another, shopping.*
- read the new word *which* on page 79 in book 2.
- check comprehension by choosing the right word to complete a sentence about a story.
- recognize the consonant blend *pl* as in *planning*.
- recognize the ending consonant blends *st* as in *just* and *ft* as in *lift*.
- review the ending *-es* after *s, sh, ch, x*.
- understand that when a consonant follows a short vowel sound, it is usually doubled before *-ing* or *-ed*.
- understand that when a word ends in silent *e*, the *e* is dropped before *-ing*, as in *come, coming*.
- understand that when a word ends in *e*, we add just *-d* instead of *ed*, as in *live, lived*.

INTRODUCTION

T: Today you will read some more stories in *City Living* and discuss the study questions in your skill book. This will be your last lesson in book 2.

I. Reading in *City Living*

STORY 3: Working in a Factory

If S. read the story at home, have him summarize it in his own words. Then go directly to the Study Helps in the skill book. If he didn't, follow the directions below.

Silent reading (pages 13–16 in *City Living*). Have S. find the story by using the table of contents, read the story title, and read the new words on each page.

Ask him to read the whole story silently to find out what Jack's job is at the factory and whether he likes his job. Record the time it takes S. to read the story. Have him answer the questions you asked.

Study helps (page 79 in book 2). Have S. read the various titles and the new word *which*. Then have him read each study question aloud and answer it. Let him scan the story to find the correct answer if he needs to.

STORY 4: City Traffic

Silent reading (pages 17–20 in *City Living*). Ask S. to read the story silently to find out what's wrong with Jimmy's car and how Jack helps him. When he has finished reading, have him give the answers.

Study helps (page 79 in skill book 2). Have S. read and answer each of the study questions.

STORY 5: At the Market

Begin this story in class, and complete it if you can. If there isn't time, you can ask S. to finish it and the other stories in *City Living* at home.

Silent reading (pages 21–23 in *City Living*). Go over the new words. Ask S. to read the story silently to find out what Ann and Jack are planning and what they do to get ready. When he has finished, discuss these questions.

Study helps (page 79 in book 2). Have S. read and answer each of the study questions. Review all of the *wh* words in the Study Helps.

CHECKUP: Page 76 in book 2

Tell S. that this Checkup is about the stories he has just read. Have him read the title and first directions. Go over the sample item with him. Then let him complete this part by himself. (If he did not finish story 5, have him do only the first five sentences.) Check his work by having him read each sentence aloud. If he missed any items, help him find the answer in the story.

Have S. read the directions for the next part of the Checkup and do it in class. Check his answers.

II. Skills Practice

T: Please close your book. We will have some exercises on consonant blends and on adding endings to words.

PRACTICE 1: Beginning Consonant Blend *pl*

T: (Write *planning*, and have S. read it.) What consonant sounds do you hear at the beginning of the word? [S: /pl/.] What letters stand for the sounds? [S: *pl*.] (Underline *pl*.) We call this the *pl* blend.

T: Which word begins with the *pl* blend as in *planning*:

plus, less?	*pain, plain?*	*play, pray?*
late, plate?	*plan, pan?*	*plenty, twenty?*

PRACTICE 2: Ending Consonant Blends *st, ft*

T: (Write *just* on the board.) Read the word. [S: just.] *Just* ends with the consonant blend *st*. (Underline *st*.)

T: Which word ends with the blend *st* as in *just*:

nest, mess?	*must, miss?*	*fast, fuss?*
pass, past?	*less, list?*	*west, risk?*

T: (Write *lift* on the board.) Read the word. [S: lift.] *Lift* ends with the consonant blend *ft*. (Underline *ft*.)

T: Which word ends with the blend *ft* as in *lift:*

sit, soft?	*left, laugh?*	*draft, bath?*
gift, get?	*draft, half?*	*shift, stiff?*

PRACTICE 3: Ending *-es*

Write *glass, box, lunch, dish* on the board. Have S. read each word and tell what it would be with the ending *-es* added. Then have him tell what letter or letters stand for the last sound in each root word [*ss, x, ch, sh*].

T: Remember, when a word ends in *s, x, ch,* or *sh,* we add the ending *-es* instead of *-s.*

T: Which ending would we add to this word, *-s* or *-es:*

pass? [S: -es.]	*hat?* [S: -s.]	*wash?* [S: -es.]
car? [S: -s.]	*tax?* [S: -es.]	*truck?* [S: -s.]
fix? [S: -es.]	*fish?* [S: -es.]	*match?* [S: -es.]

PRACTICE 4: Verb Endings *-ing, -ed*

When to double the final consonant. On the board, write these words in columns as shown here:

stop	*stopping*	*stopped*
plan	*planning*	*planned*

Have S. read all three forms of each word. Point out that *stop* and *plan* each end with a consonant with a short vowel in front of it.

T: When a root word ends in a consonant with a short vowel in front of it, you must usually double the last consonant before adding *-ing* or *-ed.*

Write *drop, shop* in column 1. Have S. tell how to write each word with *-ing* and *-ed.* As he answers, write the words in the appropriate columns.

When not to double. Write these words in columns:

pass	*passing*	*passed*
turn	*turning*	*turned*
watch	*watching*	*watched*

Have S. read all three forms of each word. Ask him to tell how many consonants each root word ends with.

T: When the root word ends with two or more consonants, you don't have to double the last consonant before *-ing* or *-ed.* Just add the ending.

Write *work, ask, kiss, match* in column 1. Have S. tell how to write each word with *-ing* and *-ed.* As he answers, write the words in the appropriate columns.

When the root word ends in silent *e*. Write these words:

live	*living*
come	*coming*

Have S. read both forms of each word. Remind him that when the root word ends in silent *e,* we drop the *e* before adding *-ing.* Write *have* and *give* in column 1. Have S. tell how to write each word with *-ing.* As he answers, write *having* and *giving* in column 2.

Write *lived* in column 3. Explain that when the root word ends in *e,* we just add *-d* instead of *-ed.* Have S. read *live, lived.* (Also, explain that we do not add *-d* to the other words in this list. Instead, we use the words *came, had, gave.* These words will be in the next book.)

III. Writing

CHECK HOMEWORK: Page 78

Check this page with S. Help him correct any errors.

WRITING LESSON: Page 81

Go over the directions and the sample item for the first part. Let S. do this part by himself. Check his work and have him correct any errors.

Follow the same procedure for the other two parts. Give any suggestions that may help S. improve his writing.

HOMEWORK: Page 82

1. Have S. look at page 82. Explain that this page is like the Writing Lesson he just did. Go over the directions with him, and ask him to do this page at home.

2. On page 83, have S. read the title *Word List.* Ask him to go over the list of words at home and see how many he can read. If he can't remember a word, he can find it in the lesson where it is first used. So that he will know how to do this, have him read the first two words in the list and tell in which lesson each word is first used. Explain that the mark * by *add* means that the word was used in the directions.

3. Ask S. to finish reading *City Living* at home. Go over the new words in the last two stories with him.

Ask S. to bring his skill book to class next time so you can go over the Homework page. Tell him that he will do a Checkup on the whole skill book next time.

CHECKING PROGRESS

In the Checkup, notice your student's ability to distinguish words as he chooses the right one to complete the sentence. If he missed some items, have him read all the words for the sentence aloud. Note the cause of his errors. Is his difficulty with word recognition, comprehension of the sentence, or remembering a fact from the stories? Does he choose the wrong word because he is judging the word from its shape or its beginning sound instead of looking at each phonetic element from left to right?

In the Skills Practice and Writing Lesson, note how well S. understands when to double the consonant before *-ing* or *-ed.* Does he understand when to use the ending *-es* instead of *-s?*

Circle one word.

	Jack and Ann live in the	market	farm	**(city)**
1.	Jack works in a	shop	**(factory)**	market
2.	Jack's job is to fill boxes with	**(glass)**	grass	skirts
3.	The city has many traffic	shops	**(cops)**	tops
4.	Jimmy's car will not	**(start)**	stop	dark
5.	Jimmy's car is in the parking	not	**(lot)**	top
6.	Jack and Ann are planning a	lunch	garden	**(dinner)**
7.	Ann and Jack get three ducks at the	**(market)**	office	farm
8.	Ann gets a jar of	apples	eggs	**(olives)**
9.	Jack gets a box of	**(matches)**	apples	jelly
10.	Ann gives the woman twenty	cents	**(dollars)**	things

Fill in the words.

1. _Jimmy_ Fisher is Jack's friend.

2. Jimmy's car has a _dead_ battery.

3. _Jack_ gives Jimmy a lift.

Copy the word. Add -ing. What is the word?

1. fill **filling**   4. fish

2. visit   5. look

3. hunt   6. work

Copy the word. Add another t and then -ing. What is the word?

1. get **getting**   4. sit

2. pet   5. put

3. cut   6. hit

Copy the word but not the e. Add -ing. What is the word?

1. come **coming**   4. live

2. have   5. write

3. give   6. name

MEETING INDIVIDUAL NEEDS

If you think S. needs more practice with sentence-completion exercises like the one in the Checkup, you may write a similar exercise for one of the shorter stories in *More Stories 2*.

If S. needs more practice on adding endings, you may prepare exercises similar to the ones in this manual.

In *More Stories 2*, the stories for Lesson 14 may be read in class or suggested for reading at home, if this will not interfere with completing *City Living*.

In *Focus on Phonics 2*, the remaining practices cover changing *y* to *i* before endings, compound words, and two-syllable words with short vowel sounds. These may be suitable at this time for an able student, but you may decide to save them for a later time.

If S. needs further practice with beginning or ending consonant blends, or with *er, ir, ur,* and *ar* words, you may want to begin using the consonant blends section of *Focus on Phonics 2*. It covers all of these skills and is designed to be used after book 2.

Copy the word. Add -ing. What is the word?

1. burn   4. say

2. jump   5. yell

3. kiss   6. kill

Copy the word. Add another t and then -ing. What is the word?

1. hit   3. pet

2. sit   4. cut

Copy the word. Add another n and then -ing. What is the word?

1. run   2. plan

Copy the word. Add another p and then -ing. What is the word?

1. shop   2. stop

Copy the word but not the e. Add -ing. What is the word?

1. come   3. give

2. have   4. live

CHECKUPS for Book 2

To evaluate the student's progress in reading and writing skills, use *Laubach Way to Reading 2 Checkups,* available on the New Readers Press website.

OBJECTIVES

The objectives of the evaluation are:

- to measure the student's progress in relation to the learning objectives of book 2.
- to diagnose the student's strengths and weaknesses in phonics, reading comprehension, and writing.
- to develop the student's confidence in taking a test.

ADMINISTERING THE CHECKUPS

The Checkups consists of five parts. Simple written directions are given for each part, and most parts have one or two sample questions. Go over the directions and samples with S. before he does each part. Help him correct any errors he makes in the samples, but do not correct his errors in the actual test items.

Introduction

T: Today you will do some checkups on book 2. They will help you find out if there are any sounds or words you need to study more. Some of the checkups will show how well you understand what you read. You will also write some words and sentences.

T: There are no new words in the checkups. And most of the checkups are like the ones you did in your skill book. So you don't need to feel nervous about doing the checkups. There is no certain score that you need to make in order to go on to book 3. But the checkups will help us know what things to give more attention to when you are studying that book.

Give S. his booklet. Read the title at the top (*Laubach Way to Reading 2 Checkups*), and have S. read it after you. Have him read the word *Name* and write his name on the line.

Checkup 1: Sound-letter relationships (pages 1–3)

S. fills in the missing letter or letters in words for sounds taught in book 2:

1. The short vowel sounds /a/, /e/, /i/, /o/, /u/ represented by *a, e, i, o, u.*
2. The vowel sound /y/ represented by *y,* as in *lily.*
3. The sound /ar/ represented by *ar.*
4. The sound /er/ represented by *er, ir, ur.*
5. The double consonants *ll, nn, ss, tt* representing a single consonant sound.
6. The sound /k/ represented by *c, k, ck.*

7. The sounds /wh/, /ng/, and voiced /th/ represented by *wh, ng,* and *th.*
8. The beginning consonant blends *cl, gl, br, dr, tr, st.*

Each word, with a blank for each missing letter, is printed next to the illustration for the word. There are 37 items and one sample.

What to do. Have S. read the title *Checkup 1* and the direction *Fill in the letters.* The items *bed* and *bell* are sample questions. For each one, have S. notice the number of blanks and what part of the word—beginning, middle, or end—is missing. Then have him say the word aloud, listen for the sound in that part of the word, and write the letter (or letters) for that part.

Let S. do the rest of page 1 by himself. Tell him that he may ask if he doesn't know what a picture is. If he asks, tell him the word, but don't emphasize the sound for the missing letter. When S. completes page 1, check to make sure he understood the directions. Then let him do pages 2–3.

Checkup 2: Adding endings (page 4)

S. adds a certain ending to the root word given and then writes the new word. He makes any changes needed in the root word before adding the ending. He adds *-s* or *-es* to six words, *-ed* to four words, and *-ing* to four words. Two samples are shown for each part of this checkup.

What to do. Have S. read the title *Checkup 2.* Tell him that this is a checkup on adding endings to words.

Add *-s* or *-es* to the word. Then write the word. Have S. read these directions and then look at the two sample items: *arm, arms* and *glass, glasses.* For each sample, have him read both words aloud and tell which ending, *-s* or *-es,* has been added to the root word. Then let him complete this part.

Add *-ed* to the word. Then write the word. Have S. read these directions and then look at the two sample items: *kiss, kissed* and *stop, stopped.* For each sample, have him read both words aloud and tell whether any change was made in the root word before the ending *-ed* was added. If he does not notice that the *p* is doubled in *stopped,* call attention to this. Then let him complete this part.

Add *-ing* to the word. Then write the word. Have S. read these directions and then look at the two sample items: *fish, fishing* and *cut, cutting.* For each sample, have him read both words aloud and tell whether any change was made in the root word before the ending *-ing* was added. If he does not notice that the *t* is doubled in *cutting,* call attention to this. Then let him complete this part.

Checkup 3: Word recognition (page 5)

S. circles one of three words to complete a sentence. There are 20 items and one sample.

What to do. Have S. read the title *Checkup 3* and the direction *Circle one word*. Have him read the sample sentence to himself, circle the right word, and then read the completed sentence aloud. Then let S. complete this page by himself. (It may help him to keep his place if he uses a strip of paper as a marker under the sentence he is working on.)

Checkup 4: Listen and write (page 6)

S. writes 10 words and 5 sentences from dictation. Sentences include the use of capital letters, periods, possessive endings -'s and -s', and question marks.

What to do. Have S. read the title *Checkup 4*. Tell him that this page is like some of the Writing Lessons in the skill book. Dictate these words for him to write:

1. black
2. clock
3. grass
4. drop
5. start
6. windy
7. plan
8. slim
9. lunch
10. which

Dictate these sentences for S. to write. Remind him to use capitals where needed and to put in the right punctuation marks.

1. That is the Hills' dinner.
2. Fern's skirt is burning.
3. Is the farmers' market in the city?
4. Are the eggs fresh?
5. Bud is Mrs. Hill's brother.

Checkup 5: Reading comprehension (pages 7–8)

S. reads a short paragraph, then answers three to five questions by circling *Yes* or *No*. There are six paragraphs with a total of 22 questions. One sample paragraph with two questions is given.

What to do. Have S. read the title *Checkup 5* and the direction *Circle Yes or No*. Have S. read the sample paragraph silently and then aloud. Have him read each question, tell whether Yes or No is the right answer, and then circle the right answer. If he doesn't give the right answer, have him find the place in the paragraph that tells the answer.

Let S. complete *Checkup 5* by himself. Give encouragement, but do not tell him any words. If he seems frustrated, don't insist on his completing this checkup. Collect his booklet when he has completed all he can.

Concluding the lesson

Tell S. that you will go over the checkups together at the next lesson. If there is time, have him read aloud from *City Living*. Ask him to finish it at home.

SCORING AND EVALUATING THE CHECKUPS

On the student's booklet, mark his *correct* answers rather than his wrong answers. Answer keys are included in the Teacher's Evaluation Form on the next page. Use this form to record his scores. Do not count the answers to sample questions. The suggested satisfactory score is about 75% of the perfect score for each part. If you want to translate the student's score into a percentage, divide his score by the perfect score and multiply by 100. The student's scores are for *your* use. The numbers would be of little use to the student.

The scores for each part of the checkups will give you an informal diagnosis of the student's strengths and weaknesses. If he made less than the suggested satisfactory score for a particular checkup, analyze the type of errors he made. List the items that he needs to review the most.

REVIEWING THE CHECKUPS WITH THE STUDENT

At your next session, go over the checkups with S. Be sure to point out his correct answers so that he receives some encouraging news about his work. Help him correct his wrong answers, as you have done with book exercises, so that he has a chance to learn from the checkups.

If S. made very few errors in the checkups, you can teach Lesson 1 of book 3 in the same session. If you need quite a bit of time to go over the checkups, spend the rest of the session reviewing. (This will give you a full lesson period to introduce Lesson 1 of book 3 at the following session.)

Plan the review around the skills that most need strengthening. Flash cards, games, and exercises in *Focus on Phonics 2* may be used for further practice. If S. needs help with beginning or ending consonant blends or with the *r*-controlled vowels, you may want to use *Focus on Phonics 2*. (It is not necessary to complete it before going on to book 3, however.)

A review lesson should contain some new reading material as well as practice on skills. Have S. complete *City Living* and *More Stories 2*. You may also want to look for other books from New Readers Press that are controlled to the book 2 vocabulary.

If you think that S. really needs an extra review lesson before going on to book 3, you may plan one. But do not hold him back unnecessarily. You can supplement the lessons in book 3 with special exercises to practice skills which need attention.

Be sure to give S. some encouraging report about his progress. Also, assure him that the checkups are only one way to measure progress. What he does in class and the use he makes of reading and writing in his daily life are even more important.

CHECKUPS FOR BOOK 2: Teacher's Evaluation Form

Student's Name _____

Date of Enrollment _____ Date Checkups Given _____

	Perfect Score	Satisfactory Score	Student's Score
1. Sound-Letter Relationships Each word completed correctly counts 1 point. (Do not count the sample items *bed* and *bell*.)	36	27	
2. Adding Endings Each word written correctly with the ending counts as 1 point.	14	10	
3. Word Recognition 1. sister 5. picture 9. office 13. start 17. building 2. kitchen 6. stuck 10. dollars 14. curtains 18. son 3. dinner 7. bed 11. bag 15. farm 19. black 4. city 8. friends 12. path 16. person 20. fun	20	15	
4. Listen and Write Count 1 point for each *word* spelled correctly. 1. black 3. grass 5. start 7. plan 9. lunch 2. clock 4. drop 6. windy 8. slim 10. which Count 3 points for each sentence written correctly, as follows: —1 point if a capital letter is used at the beginning of the sentence. —1 point for correct spelling of all words, including correct use of capital letters on names and correct placement of apostrophe. —1 point for correct end punctuation —period or question mark. 1. That is the Hills' dinner. 4. Are the eggs fresh? 2. Fern's skirt is burning. 5. Bud is Mrs. Hill's brother. 3. Is the farmers' market in the city?	25	19	
5. Reading Comprehension Each correct answer counts 1 point. Sample Set 1 Set 2 Set 3 Set 4 Set 5 Set 6 Do 1. No 1. No 1. Yes 1. No 1. No 1. No 4. Yes not 2. Yes 2. Yes 2. No 2. No 2. Yes 2. Yes 5. No count. 3. No 3. No 3. Yes 3. Yes 3. No 3. No 4. Yes 4. Yes	22	16	
Total Score	**117**	**87**	

Word List for Book 2

Laubach Way to Reading 2 and its correlated reader *City Living* introduce the 262 words listed below, including 217 different words and 45 variants. Root words are listed as main entries. Variants with -*s* and -'*s* (possessive) are not listed. Variants with -*s'*, -*es*, -*ing*, -*ed*, and -*er* (comparative) are usually indented, but if only a variant is introduced, it is listed as a main entry. When the variant is in italics, the root word was introduced in book 1.

Words introduced in titles and directions are starred. The number indicates the lesson in which the word is introduced. The abbreviation *cr* stands for correlated reader.

13	* add	8	cat	11	father
9	after	6	cent	11	fern
cr	another	cr	center	2	* fill
cr	any	10	Chan	15	— filling
12	arm	14	* circle	1	finger
12	Arthur	3	city	11	first
cr	ask	10	clock	3	Fisher
8	back	14	color	cr	fit
cr	bad	5	come	10	fix
cr	badly	cr	— coming	6	Fred
8	bag	cr	cop	6	fresh
12	barn	13	* copy	7	friend
8	basket	11	cover	5	from
8	bat	11	— covered	cr	fun
cr	battery	11	curtain	5	funny
7	bed	4	cut	12	garden
6	bell	4	— cutting	1	— *getting*
11	better	cr	dad	1	gift
1	big	12	dark	1	— *giving*
8	black	cr	dead	9	glass
cr	— *boxes*	cr	did	10	got
cr	bread	2	dinner	9	grass
5	brick	10	doctor	4	gun
4	bring	5	does	9	half
2	—bringing	10	doll	cr	happened
5	brother	10	dollar	8	happy
5	Buck	10	Don	12	hard
5	Bud	10	Dr.	cr	hat
3	building	cr	dress	cr	— *having*
11	burn	cr	— dresses	10	head
11	— burned	cr	drop	11	heard
11	— burning	10	— dropped	6	help
cr	but	4	duck	11	— helping
cr	butter	6	Ellen	6	hen
8	can	9	factory	2	—*Hills'*
8	cannot	8	family	4	hit
12	car	12	far	10	hot
12	Carl	12	farm	4	hunting
12	Carmen	12	farmer	11	hurry
cr	carry	cr	fast	11	— hurried
8	— carrying	cr	— faster	cr	into

1	it	11	nurse	cr	— started
8	Jack	10	office	12	— starting
12	jar	14	* or	cr	stitches
12	jelly	cr	other	cr	— stitched
3	Jimmy	cr	park	10	stop
10	job	12	— parking	10	— stopped
10	John	cr	pass	cr	— stopping
cr	just	cr	— passes	5	stuck
8	kill	cr	past	1	* study
3	King	9	path	4	sun
cr	kiss	11	person	8	that
cr	— kisses	11	— picked	7	them
cr	— kissing	3	picture	11	then
2	kitchen	cr	pink	cr	thing
3	Kitty	15	plan	5	think
12	large	cr	— planning	cr	— thinking
9	laugh	3	pretty	10	Tom
cr	— laughed	cr	puppy	10	top
cr	— laughing	8	quick	cr	traffic
cr	left	7	quickly	5	truck
cr	let	11	ran	cr	turn
12	— let's	8	rat	6	twelve
2	* letter	cr	ready	cr	twenty
cr	lift	7	red	11	us
3	lily	1	ring	6	very
cr	list	10	rock	11	was
1	little	11	rug	cr	watches
cr	— living	11	— running	cr	— watching
10	lock	11	said	7	well
11	— looked	7	send	cr	went
cr	lot	cr	seven	11	were
9	lunch	6	seventy	13	what
6	many	cr	— shopping	cr	when
cr	marked	10	shot	15	which
12	market	7	sick	2	whistle
8	marry	2	singing	14	who
cr	— married	1	sister	6	will
11	match	7	sit	3	windy
cr	— matches	2	— sitting	2	with
7	men	cr	six	7	women
11	Miller	11	skirt	2	* word
1	Miss	cr	slim	12	work
10	Molly	8	Smith	12	— working
5	mother	5	some	11	— yelled
3	Ms.	4	son	11	— yelling
4	mud	8	standing		
cr	must	12	start		